Drones, Surveillance, and Targeted Killings

Other Books in the Current Controversies Series:

Drones, Surveillance, and Targeted Killings

Anne Cunningham, Book Editor

GREENHAVEN
PUBLISHING

Published in 2017 by Greenhaven Publishing, LLC
353 3rd Avenue, Suite 255, New York, NY 10010

Articles in Greenhaven Publishing anthologies are often edited for length to meet page
requirements. In addition, original titles of these works are changed to clearly present
the main thesis and to explicitly indicate the author's opinion. Every effort is made to
ensure that Greenhaven Publishing accurately reflects the original intent of the authors.
Every effort has been made to trace the owners of the copyrighted material.

Cover image: Ivan Cholakov / Shutterstock.com

Library of Congress Cataloging-in-Publication Data

Names: Cunningham, Anne.
Title: Drones, surveillance, and targeted killings / Anne Cunningham.
Description: New York : Greenhaven Publishing, 2017. |
Series: Current controversies | Includes index.
Identifiers: LCCN ISBN 9781534500365 (pbk.) | ISBN 9781534500204 (library bound)
Subjects: LCSH: Drone aircraft—Juvenile literature. | Air pilots,
Military—United States—Juvenile literature.
Classification: LCC UG1242.D7 C75 2017 | DDC 623.74'69—dc23

Manufactured in the United States of America

Website: http://greenhavenpublishing.com

Contents

Chapter 1: Should the United States Continue to Engage in Drone Warfare?

Christopher Olver

Unmanned aerial vehicles (UAVs), commonly known as drones, offer the military and intelligence communities powerful tools for counter-terrorism surveillance and targeting strikes, but all too frequent civilian casualties raise serious ethical concerns of killing by remote.

Yes: Drones Help the US Military Avoid
Casualties and Achieve Strategic Goals

Wayne McLean

Economic analysis has historically determined military expenditures. For this reason, drones will remain in use because they currently offer greater value and efficacy than "boots on the ground." This makes their drawbacks comparatively less important.

Neve Gordon

Drones are changing how war is waged in several important ways. They project power without rendering soldiers vulnerable, aid in surveillance, and allow precise targeting of enemy combatants.

No: Drone Strikes Radicalize Victimized
Populations and Violate International Law

Andrew Callam

Drones have sharpened US counter-insurgency efforts, but their use for "hunter-killer" CIA missions may violate international law and arguably creates more terrorists. Furthermore, the perception that drones are costless and risk free might lead to endless war rather than diplomacy.

military-style technology are not suitable or necessary for the primary job of peaceful border administration.

The Use of UAVs on the Border
Should Be Discontinued
Arthur Holland Michel
The drones used on the large US border with Mexico replaced a failed program to monitor inaccessible areas. However, according to an audit of the drone program, it has not fared much better. Crashes, limited flight hours, and expense make for an unwieldy program that could be a waste of taxpayer resources.

Border Drones Are Costly and Ineffective
Tom Barry
Evaluations of the US government's drone program reveal that drones do not contribute to a more secure border. In addition, the relatively meager results of the drone program do not merit the tremendous funding the government is pouring into it.

Chapter 3: Should Drones Be Used for Domestic Surveillance?

Overview: Responses to the Domestic
Drone Surveillance Program
ACLU of Massachusetts
As surveillance drones have become more common, advocates for civil liberties and privacy have advanced legislation seeking to limit their power. Meanwhile, law enforcement agencies are eager to exploit this new technology, raising additional concerns about an increasingly militarized police force.

Yes: Drones Help Reduce Illegal Activity and
Keep Americans Safe

Drones Can Benefit Civilians and
Monitor Human Rights Abuses
Sarah Stein Kerr
Contrary to popular belief, drones can have peaceful, positive applications. For example, they can be used to monitor human

rights abuses in remote locations. However, the possibility of privacy violation requires checks and oversight on such uses.

As drones become more common in everyday life, proper regulation is also essential. The Obama administration and the FAA have taken some initial steps on this front, but critics say not enough is being done to prevent violations of privacy and other potential infringements on individual rights.

No: Checks Against the Potentially Dangerous and Invasive Uses of Drones Are Required

Drones provide the government with a powerful tool for surveillance and gathering information. Some argue this can violate Fourth Amendment protections against unreasonable search and seizure. Here, Senator Rand Paul argues that under most circumstances, drones must obtain warrants.

Common law defines how airspace that is neither fully public nor private is regulated. Many are concerned with the privacy invading potential of drones and are thus recommending stricter definitions by the courts, as well as binding voluntary guidelines for drone operators.

Chapter 4: Are Civilian Drones a Danger to Society?

Plenty of groups and individuals are vocal about their opposition to armed drones abroad. But opinions regarding the use of surveillance drones domestically are much more muted. The welcoming by Congress of unmanned aerial vehicles in US airspace has resulted in increasingly crowded skies. But should Americans be wary?

Foreword

"Controversy" is a word that has an undeniably unpleasant connotation. It carries a definite negative charge. Controversy can spoil family gatherings, spread a chill around classroom and campus discussion, inflame public discourse, open raw civic wounds, and lead to the ouster of public officials. We often feel that controversy is almost akin to bad manners, a rude and shocking eruption of that which must not be spoken or thought of in polite, tightly guarded society. To avoid controversy, to quell controversy, is often seen as a public good, a victory for etiquette, perhaps even a moral or ethical imperative.

Yet the studious, deliberate avoidance of controversy is also a whitewashing, a denial, a death threat to democracy. It is a false sterilizing and sanitizing and superficial ordering of the messy, ragged, chaotic, at times ugly processes by which a healthy democracy identifies and confronts challenges, engages in passionate debate about appropriate approaches and solutions, and arrives at something like a consensus and a broadly accepted and supported way forward. Controversy is the megaphone, the speaker's corner, the public square through which the citizenry finds and uses its voice. Controversy is the lifeblood of our democracy and absolutely essential to the vibrant health of our society.

Our present age is certainly no stranger to controversy. We are consumed by fierce debates about technology, privacy, political correctness, poverty, violence, crime and policing, guns, immigration, civil and human rights, terrorism, militarism, environmental protection, and gender and racial equality. Loudly competing voices are raised every day, shouting opposing opinions, putting forth competing agendas, and summoning starkly different visions of a utopian or dystopian future. Often these voices attempt to shout the others down; there is precious little listening and considering among the cacophonous din. Yet listening and considering, too, are essential to the health of a democracy. If controversy is democracy's lusty lifeblood, respectful listening and careful thought are its higher faculties, its brain, its conscience.

Current Controversies does not shy away from or attempt to hush the loudly competing voices. It seeks to provide readers with as wide and representative as possible a range of articulate voices on any given controversy of the day, separates each one out to allow it to be heard clearly and fairly, and encourages careful listening to each of these well-crafted, thoughtfully expressed opinions, supplied by some of today's leading academics, thinkers, analysts, politicians, policy makers, economists, activists, change agents, and advocates. Only after listening to a wide range of opinions on an issue, evaluating the strengths and weaknesses of each argument, assessing how well the facts and available evidence mesh with the stated opinions and conclusions, and thoughtfully and critically examining one's own beliefs and conscience can the reader begin to arrive at his or her own conclusions and articulate his or her own stance on the spotlighted controversy.

This process is facilitated and supported in each Current Controversies volume by an introduction and chapter overviews that provide readers with the essential context they need to begin engaging with the spotlighted controversies, with the debates surrounding them, and with their own perhaps shifting or nascent opinions on them. Chapters are organized around several key questions that are answered with diverse opinions representing all points on the political spectrum. In its content, organization, and methodology, readers are encouraged to determine the authors' point of view and purpose, interrogate and analyze the various arguments and their rhetoric and structure, evaluate the arguments' strengths and weaknesses, test their claims against available facts and evidence, judge the validity of the reasoning, and bring into clearer, sharper focus the reader's own beliefs and conclusions and how they may differ from or align with those in the collection or those of classmates.

Research has shown that reading comprehension skills improve dramatically when students are provided with compelling, intriguing, and relevant "discussable" texts. The subject matter of these collections could not be more compelling, intriguing, or urgently relevant to today's students and the world they are poised to inherit. The anthologized articles also provide the basis for stimulating, lively, and passionate classroom debates. Students who are compelled to anticipate objections to their own argument and identify the flaws in those of an opponent read more carefully, think more critically, and steep themselves in relevant context, facts, and information more thoroughly. In short, using discussable text of the kind provided by every single volume in the Current Controversies series encourages close reading, facilitates reading comprehension, fosters research, strengthens critical thinking, and greatly enlivens and energizes classroom discussion and participation. The entire learning process is deepened, extended, and strengthened.

If we are to foster a knowledgeable, responsible, active, and engaged citizenry, we must provide readers with the intellectual, interpretive, and critical-thinking tools and experience necessary to make sense of the world around them and of the all-important debates and arguments that inform it. We must encourage them not to run away from or attempt to quell controversy but to embrace it in a responsible, conscientious, and thoughtful way, to sharpen and strengthen their own informed opinions by listening to and critically analyzing those of others. This series encourages respectful engagement with and analysis of current controversies and competing opinions and fosters a resulting increase in the strength and rigor of one's own opinions and stances. As such, it helps readers assume their rightful place in the public square and provides them with the skills necessary to uphold their awesome responsibility—guaranteeing the continued and future health of a vital, vibrant, and free democracy.

Introduction

U nmanned aerial vehicles (UAVs), or "drones" as they are more commonly known, are a booming industry—and a nexus for controversial debate within contemporary political and legal discourse. As with much powerful new technology, drones present a confluence of practical uses and potential abuses in both military and civilian life. As such, the rules and regulation of UAVs are a work in progress. These laws seek to balance drones' enormous potential with their frighteningly invasive and destructive capabilities.

The earliest known drones took flight in the mid-nineteenth century, primarily for military use. Fittingly, when we think today of drones, we generally picture the technologically sophisticated, expensive, and deadly UAVs deployed overseas by the US military. Since 2008, the Obama administration has been credited (and vociferously criticized) for using drones as the centerpiece of a highly aggressive counterterrorism strategy. While there is no question that targeted drone strikes have been instrumental in disabling terrorist networks such as al-Qaeda, questions of international law, due process, and proper oversight haunt nearly every drone strike. More troublingly, there is ample evidence that US drones have murdered a significant amount of civilians. Opponents of military drones claim that their use is arguably the most powerful recruitment for ISIS and other radical non-state organizations. For every insurgent killed, several more are perhaps seeking to avenge the death of an innocent loved one, incinerated from above by a US Hellfire missile.

If aerial strikes are potentially counterproductive in the long-term, why has the US military chosen to double down on drone warfare? The obvious reason is that drones expose US soldiers to far less risk than a "boots on the ground" strategy. Moreover, drones are capable of relaying a constant stream of surveillance data that is crucial for the intelligence community. Analysts calculate that despite the considerable per flight hour cost of UAVs such as the Reaper and Predator, drones still represent a relative bargain compared to the overhead of deploying soldiers, especially once the cost of often lifelong medical care is factored into the equation. In short, hawks contend that drones project immense power, with little risk or cost. Thus, UAVs offer the cash-strapped military the best "bang for their buck." On the other hand, if the bar of entry for armed conflict is merely flying a remote control bomber into enemy territory, many critics suggest this does not bode well for peace, diplomacy, and global stability.

Drones have peacetime applications as well, but these too are controversial. On the domestic governmental front, the Department of Homeland Security, US Customs and Border Protection, and even local law enforcement are now looking to drones as a way to do their jobs more efficiently. As we will see from the reporting to follow, the verdict as to whether these efforts have been successful is mixed. Proponents of drone patrols along the southern US border cite significant drug busts, while skeptics regard them as flashy toys, ill-suited to the rather mundane work of border patrol. While cost-benefit analyses present some mixed evidence, many credible reporters have concluded that using drones in these contexts is a waste of taxpayer resources. Advocates for increased peacetime drone use have suggested humanitarian applications such as disaster relief and human rights monitoring in remote villages. Whether such drone use will conform to the needs of private military subcontractors and other commercial manufacturers remains to be seen.

As the drone industry has exploded, hobbyists are purchasing drones for personal use. Amateur drone piloting has raised thorny questions of individual liberty and privacy, as concerned citizens worry their privacy will be violated, either through overt spying or through the collection of data such as cellular signals and location. In response, the Federal Aviation Administration (FAA) has recently issued rules requiring that all drones be registered and that they stay under 400 feet (121 meters) in altitude and within sight distance of the operator. DJI, a leading commercial drone manufacturer, has instituted a feature called "geofencing" to keep drones away from airports and other sensitive locations. Some drone owners oppose this basic public safety measure, claiming it is an intrusion into fair use of personal property.

As an inherently neutral technology, the ways in which drones are used reflect societal values. Similarly, concern and borderline paranoia over drones may speak to uniquely American preoccupations with individual freedoms and privacy. The viewpoints contained in *Current Controversies: Drones, Surveillance, and Targeted Killings* arrive at different conclusions on drone use, typically reflecting the priorities and biases of each author. Readers are encouraged to not only draw conclusions about drones, but to understand what these conclusions mean in a larger political and ideological context.

CHAPTER 1

Should the United States Continue to Engage in Drone Warfare?

Overview: Drone Strikes Offer Solutions and Dangers

Christopher Olver

Christopher Olver was founding content editor at Journalist's Resource.

From the program's inception in 2004 through early 2013, estimates put the number of militant deaths from 350 reported drone strikes in Pakistan between 1,533 and 2,658, according to the New America Foundation's drones database. That research project finds that the "average non-militant casualty rate over the life of the program is 18-23 percent. In 2012 it was around 10 percent, down sharply from its peak in 2006 of almost 100 percent." In addition, some 61 drone strikes have now taken place in Yemen.

As scholars note, the U.S. program retains broad support politically and its relative ease of use—versus the deployment of ground troops into dangerous situations—may make the use of force in general more likely; a Washington Post/ABC News poll in 2012 found that 83 percent of respondents either strongly or "somewhat" approved of its use against overseas terrorist suspects. Further, a 2013 Pew Research Center survey found that "56% approve of the U.S. conducting missile strikes from pilotless aircraft to target extremists in countries such as Pakistan, Yemen and Somalia; just 26% say they disapprove."

A 2011 paper from researchers at CUNY Graduate Center and the Institute for the Study of Labor in Bonn, Germany, "Are Drone Strikes Effective in Afghanistan and Pakistan? On the Dynamics of Violence between the United States and the Taliban," uses the Worldwide Incidents Tracking System (WITS) database to understand the context of drone strikes in Afghanistan and Pakistan between January 2007 and December 2010 and to determine their impact on terrorist violence.

According to the New America Foundation data on which the study is based, in 2010 there were 118 drone strikes in Pakistan, of which 14 were successful. (Success was defined as a strike in which a militant leader was killed.) By comparison, in 2009 there were 53 strikes in the country, nine of which were successful. Drone strikes are thought to affect those targeted in three ways: First, they can lead to the depletion or incapacitation of enemy ranks; second, they can deter future attacks; third, they can produce a "vengeance effect," where targeted groups are spurred to commit further acts of violence.

The study's findings include:

- In general "drone strikes matter, but only for Taliban violence in Pakistan. There is little or no [statistically significant] effect of drone strikes on Taliban violence across the border in Afghanistan."
- The impact in Pakistan "varies from a positive vengeance effect in the first week following a drone strike to a negative deterrent/incapacitation effect in the second week following a drone strike, when we examine the incidence of terrorist attacks by the Taliban. The impact is negative in both the first and second week following a drone strike, when we examine the number of terrorist attacks by the Taliban."
- A terrorist attack by the Taliban in Pakistan is 8.2% more likely to occur five days after a drone strike but 8.9% less likely to occur 13 days after a drone strike.
- A terrorist attack in Pakistan is 17.8% less likely to occur three days after a successful drone strike; and a terrorist attack in Pakistan is 13% less likely to occur 12 days after an unsuccessful drone strike.
- "There is no large and significant impact of unsuccessful drone strikes on terrorist attacks by the Taliban in Afghanistan, but a terrorist attack in Afghanistan is 8.8% more likely five days

after a successful drone strike. This indicates that vengeance effects may be particularly strong when drone strikes are able to kill militant leaders for Taliban violence in Afghanistan."

"We find some vengeance effects of drone strikes on violence by the Haqqani faction [of the Taliban] but also deterrent/ incapacitation effects of drone strikes on violence by both the Haqqani and Mehsud factions of the Taliban," the researchers conclude. "We estimate the differential effects of successful and unsuccessful drone strikes (which kill and do not kill a militant leader) on Taliban violence in Afghanistan and in Pakistan. We find strong negative impacts of unsuccessful drone strikes on Taliban violence in Pakistan, showing the deterrent effects of drone strikes are quite strong while the incapacitation effects of drone strikes are weak or non-existent."

A 2013 paper from Harvard's Shorenstein Center, "Media Coverage of the Drone Program," explores and tracks news reports on the issue and finds that critical reporting has increased in recent years.

The Benefits of Drones Greatly Outweigh the Costs

Wayne McLean

Wayne McLean is a PhD candidate with the National Security College at Australian National University and previously an associate lecturer in international relations at the University of Tasmania. His research focuses on the foreign policy of middle powers with a focus on Turkey, Central Asia, and Australia.

Cost is largely absent in the key debates around the use of unmanned drones in war, even though drones are a cost-effective way of achieving national security objectives.

Many of the common objections to drones, such as their ambiguous place in humanitarian law, become second-tier issues when the cost benefits are laid out. For strategic military planners, cost efficiencies mean that economic outputs can be more effectively translated into hard military power. This means that good intentions concerned with restricting the use of drones are likely to remain secondary.

This pattern of cost-trumping-all has historical precedents. The cheap English longbow rendered the expensive (but "honourable") horse-and-knight combination redundant in the 14th century. Later, the simple and cost-effective design of the machine gun changed centuries of European military doctrine in just a few years.

Drones are cheap

These basic principles are visible in the emergence of drones. For example, according to the American Security Project, unclassified reports show that the MQ-9 Reaper drone used for attacks in

"Drones Are Cheap, Soldiers Are Not: A Cost-Benefit Analysis Of War," Wayne McLean, The Conversation, June 25, 2014. https://theconversation.com/drones-are-cheap-soldiers-are-not-a-cost-benefit-analysis-of-war-27924. Licensed under CC BY ND 4.0 International.

Pakistan has a single unit cost of US$6.48 million and an operational cost of close to US$3 million.

This latter figure is deceptive, however, as a full drone "system" requires a larger infrastructure to operate. Therefore, a typical reaper drone in a group of four on an active mission requires two active pilots, a ground station, and a secured data link. However, even with this significant infrastructure requirement the end cost is US$3250 per hour of flight time.

In contrast, the F-35 Joint Strike Fighter—which the Australian government recently announced it will buy 58 more of—costs nearly US$91 million per unit, almost US$5 million per year to operate and $16,500 per hour of flight.

While drones will never completely replace soldiers, this debate is becoming less important in the current strategic climate. The operating environments where drones are deployed—countries such as Pakistan, Somalia and Yemen—do not emphasise "hearts and minds" strategies where the human element has traditionally been valued as a force multiplier.

Instead, objectives in these countries involve attacks on specific individuals, with operational data obtained by signal intelligence beforehand. Human contact becomes even less desirable given that a key tactic of combatants in these weak states is attrition with the aim of creating low-level civil conflicts. The end goal of these actions is to inflict high economic costs to the adversary.

As a result, this remote and analytical method of engaging militarily leads to substantial cost efficiencies.

Soldiers are expensive

While military budgets get smaller, the cost of the human soldier remains expensive. For example, each US solider deployed in Afghanistan in 2012 cost the government US$2.1 million.

These costs are only part of the picture, though. Thanks to medical advances, soldiers are now more likely to survive catastrophic battleground injuries than in the past. For instance, during the Iraq and Afghan operations there were seven injuries to each fatality compared to 2.3 in World War Two and 3.8 in World War One.

This increasing likelihood of survival means a greater need for long-term support of veterans. US operations in the Middle East over the past 13 years have resulted in 1558 major limb amputations and 118,829 cases of post-traumatic stress disorder. There have also been 287,911 episodes of traumatic brain injury, often caused by a soldier's close proximity to mortar attacks.

The most serious of these injuries can incur more than 50 years of rehabilitation and medical costs, with most victims in their early 20s. For example a typical "polytrauma," where a soldier has experienced multiple traumatic injuries, has a calculated annual health care cost of US$136,000.

When rehabilitative hardware such as bionic legs is added— which can cost up to US$150,000—the expeditures are considerable over a lifetime. These costs also peak 30 years after conflict and therefore are rarely viewed in context of current operations.

Less severe and less obvious disabilities are even more frequent. Towards the end of 2012, 50% of US veterans from Iraq and Afghanistan (over 780,000), had filed disability claims ranging from military sexual trauma to mesothelioma.

On top of this there are further hidden social costs: veterans account for 20% of US suicides, nearly 50,000 veterans are at risk of homelessness, and one in eight veterans between 2006 and 2008 were referred to counsellors for alcohol abuse.

When these costs are combined, future medical outlay for veterans of the Iraq and Afghan missions are estimated to be US$836.1 billion. In this context, the benefits of solider-less modes of operation to military planners are clear.

Clear choice

From this, we can see how the move towards drones is driven by cost. The US in particular is aware of the danger of choosing "guns over butter," the economic analogy where there is always a trade-off between investment in defence and domestic prosperity.

The US used this to its advantage in the Cold War when the Soviet leadership leaned too heavily towards "guns" by spending around 25% of its budget on defence in the early 1980s. As a result, the domestic economy collapsed and any defensive gains from increased spending were lost.

America's adversaries are also acquainted with this economic tactic. Osama bin Laden and al-Qaeda's broader strategy was not to inflict damage to the US for the sake of damage itself. Rather, terrorism was part of a larger strategy of "bleeding America to the point of bankruptcy."

At the same time, China has been careful not to engage the US in a game of defence spending. It has been prudent in its expenditure, outlaying only 2.2% of its GDP on defence compared to 4.4% for the US. It is also focusing on a steady, rather than rapid collection of "traditional" defence tools, such as a blue water navy. This is because China is emphasising modernisation using new technology rather than the old metric of simple platform numbers.

From this perspective, it seems US military planners have realised the perils of overspending. Drones are viewed as the remedy. Whether this contributes to or harms international stability is yet to be seen.

Drones Are Changing Our Conception of Warfare

Neve Gordon

Neve Gordon is a professor of politics and government at Ben-Gurion University of the Negev, who writes on issues relating to the Israeli-Palestinian conflict and human rights.

This Christmas small drones were among the most popular gift under the tree in the U.S. with manufacturers stating that they sold 200,000 new unmanned aerial vehicles during the holiday season. While the rapid infiltration of drones into the gaming domain clearly reflects that drones are becoming a common weapon among armed forces, their appearance in Walmart, Toys "R" Us and Amazon serves, in turn, to normalize their deployment in the military.

Drones, as Grégoire Chamayou argues in his new book, *A Theory of the Drone,* have a uniquely seductive power, one that attracts militaries, politicians and citizens alike. A research scholar in philosophy at the Centre National de la Recherche Scientifique in Paris, Chamayou is one of the most profound contemporary thinkers working on the deployment of violence and its ethical ramifications. And while his new book offers a concise history of drones, it focuses on how drones are changing warfare and their potential to alter the political arena of the countries that utilize them.

Chamayou traces one of the central ideas informing the production and deployment of drones back to John W. Clark, an American engineer who carried out a study on "remote control in hostile environments" in 1964. In Clark's study, space is divided into two kinds of zones—hostile and safe—while robots

"Drones and the New Ethics of War," Neve Gordon, Common Dreams, January 23, 2015. http://www.commondreams.org/views/2015/01/23/drones-and-new-ethics-war. Licensed under CC-SA 3.0.

operated by remote control are able to relieve human beings of all perilous occupations within hostile zones. The sacrifice of miners, firefighters, or those working on skyscrapers will no longer be necessary, since the collapse of a tunnel in the mines, for example, would merely lead to the loss of several robots operated by remote control.

The same logic informed the creation of drones. They were initially utilized as part of the military's defense system in hostile territories. After the Egyptian military shot down about 30 Israel fighter jets in the first hours of the 1973 war, Israeli air-force commanders decided to change their tactics and send a wave of drones. As soon as the Egyptians fired their initial salvo of anti-aircraft missiles at the drones, the Israeli airplanes were able to attack as the Egyptians were reloading.

Over the years, drones have also become an important component of the intelligence revolution. Instead of sending spies or reconnaissance airplanes across enemy lines, drones can continuously fly above hostile terrain gathering information. As Chamayou explains, drones do not merely provide a constant image of the enemy, but manage to fuse together different forms of data. They carry technology that can interpret electronic communications from radios, cell phones and other devices and can link a telephone call with a particular video or provide the GPS coordinates of the person using the phone. Their target is, in other words, constantly visible.

Using drones to avert missiles or for reconnaissance was, of course, considered extremely important, yet military officials aspired to transform drones into lethal weapons as well. On February 16, 2001, after many years of U.S. investment in R&D, a Predator drone first successfully fired a missile and hit its target. As Chamayou puts it, the notion of turning the Predator into a predator had finally been realized. Within a year, the Predator was preying on live targets in Afghanistan.

A Humanitarian Weapon

Over the past decade, the United States has manufactured more than 6000 drones of various kinds. 160 of these are Predators, which are used not only in Afghanistan but also in countries officially at peace with the US, such as Yemen, Somalia and Pakistan. In Pakistan, CIA drones carry out an average of one strike every four days. Although exact figures of fatalities are difficult to establish, the estimated number of deaths between 2004 and 2012 vary from 2562 to 3325.

Chamayou underscores how drones are changing our conception of war in three major ways. First, the idea of a frontier or battlefield is rendered meaningless as is the idea that there are particular places—like homesteads—where the deployment of violence is considered criminal. In other words, if once the legality of killing was dependent on where the killing was carried out, today US lawyers argue that the traditional connection between geographical spaces—such as the battlefield, home, hospital, mosque—and forms of violence are out of date. Accordingly, every place becomes a potential site of drone violence.

Second, the development of "precise missiles," the kind with which most drones are currently armed led to the popular conception that drones are precise weapons. Precision, though, is a slippery concept. For one, chopping off a person's head with a machete is much more precise than any missile, but there is no political or military support for precision of this kind in the West. Indeed, "precision" turns out to be an extremely copious category. The U.S., for example, counts all military age males in a strike zone as combatants unless there is explicit intelligence proving them innocent posthumously. The real ruse, then, has to do with the relation between precision and geography. As precise weapons, drones also render geographical contours irrelevant since the ostensible precision of these weapons justifies the killing of suspected terrorists in their homes. A legal strike zone is then equated with anywhere the drone strikes. And when "legal killing" can occur anywhere, then one can execute suspects anywhere—even in zones traditionally conceived as off-limits.

Finally, drones change our conception of war because it becomes, in Chamayou's words, a priori impossible to die as one kills. One air-force officer formulated this basic benefit in the following manner: "The real advantage of unmanned aerial systems is that they allow you to protect power without projecting vulnerability." Consequently, drones are declared to be a humanitarian weapon in two senses: they are precise vis-à-vis the enemy, and ensure no human cost to the perpetrator.

From Conquest to Pursuit

If Guantanamo was the icon of President George W. Bush's anti-terror policy, drones have become the emblem of the Obama presidency. Indeed, Chamayou maintains that President Barack Obama has adopted a totally different anti-terror doctrine from his predecessor: kill rather than capture, replace torture with targeted assassinations.

Citing a New York Times report, Chamayou describes the way in which deadly decisions are reached: "It is the strangest of bureaucratic rituals...Every week or so, more than 100 members of the sprawling national security apparatus gather by secure video teleconference, to pore over terrorist suspects' biographies and to recommend to the president who should be the next to die." In D.C, this is called "Terror Tuesday." Once established, the list is subsequently sent to the White House where the president gives his oral approval for each name. "With the kill list validated, the drones do the rest."

Obama's doctrine entails a change in the paradigm of warfare. In contrast to military theorist Carl Von Clausewitz, who claimed that the fundamental structure of war is a duel of two fighters facing each other, we now have, in Chamayou's parlance, a hunter closing in on its a prey. Chamayou, who also wrote *Manhunts: A Philosophical History*, which examines the history of hunting humans from ancient Sparta to the modern practices of chasing undocumented migrants, recounts how according to English common law one could hunt badgers and foxes in another man's land, "because destroying such creatures is said to be profitable to the Public." This is precisely the kind of law that the US would like to claim for drones, he asserts.

The strategy of militarized manhunting is essentially preemptive. It is not a matter of responding to actual attacks but rather preventing the possibility of emerging threats by the early elimination of potential adversaries. According to this new logic, war is no longer based on conquest—Obama is not interested in colonizing swaths of land in northern Pakistan—but on the right of pursuit. The right to pursue the prey wherever it may be found, in turn, transforms the way we understand the basic principles of international relations since it undermines the notion of territorial integrity as well as the idea of nonintervention and the broadly accepted definition of sovereignty as the supreme authority over a given territory.

Wars Without Risks

The transformation of Clausewitz's warfare paradigm manifests itself in other ways as well. Drone wars are wars without losses or defeats, but they are also wars without victory. The combination of the two lays the ground for perpetual violence, the utopian fantasy of those profiting from the production of drones and similar weapons.

Just as importantly, drones change the ethics of war. According to the new military morality, to kill while exposing one's life to danger is bad; to take lives without ever endangering one's own is good. Bradley Jay Strawser, a professor of philosophy at the US naval Postgraduate school in California, is a prominent spokesperson of the "principle of unnecessary risk." It is, in his view, wrong to command someone to take an unnecessary risk, and consequently it becomes a moral imperative to deploy drones.

Exposing the lives of one's troops was never considered good, but historically it was believed to be necessary. Therefore dying for one's country was deemed to be the greatest sacrifice and those who did die were recognized as heroes. The drone wars, however, are introducing a risk-free ethics of killing. What is taking place is a switch from an ethics of "self-sacrifice and courage to one of self-preservation and more or less assumed cowardice."

Chamayou refers to this as "necro-ethics." Paradoxically, necro-ethics is, on the one hand, vitalist in the sense that the drone supposedly does not kill innocent bystanders while securing the life of the perpetrator. This has far-reaching implications, since the more ethical the weapon seems, the more acceptable it is and the more readily it will likely be used. On the other hand, the drone advances the doctrine of killing well, and in this sense stands in opposition to the classical ethics of living well or even dying well.

Transforming Politics in the Drone States

Moreover, drones change politics within the drone states. Because drones transform warfare into a ghostly teleguided act orchestrated from a base in Nevada or Missouri, whereby soldiers no longer risk their lives, the critical attitude of citizenry towards war is also profoundly transformed, altering, as it were, the political arena within drone states.

Drones, Chamayou says, are a technological solution for the inability of politicians to mobilize support for war. In the future, politicians might not need to rally citizens because once armies begin deploying only drones and robots there will be no need for the public to even know that a war is being waged. So while, on the one hand, drones help produce the social legitimacy towards warfare through the reduction of risk, on the other hand, they render social legitimacy irrelevant to the political decision making process relating to war. This drastically reduces the threshold for resorting to violence, so much so that violence appears increasingly as a default option for foreign policy. Indeed, the transformation of wars into a risk free enterprise will render them even more ubiquitous than they are today. This too will be one of Obama's legacies.

The United States Should Use Drones More Selectively

Andrew Callam

Andrew Callam earned a master's degree in international affairs from George Washington University and worked as a researcher at the National Security Archive.

On August 5, 2009, two Hellfire missiles fired from an American Predator drone crashed through the roof of a house in northwest Pakistan. Lying on the roof of his father-in-law's house was Baitullah Mehsud, the leader of the Pakistani Taliban. Along with Mehsud, the explosion killed his father-in-law, his mother-in-law, his wife, his uncle, a lieutenant and seven bodyguards.

It took three days for mainstream news sources to confirm rumors of the Taliban leader's death as the Taliban moved to prevent the news from leaking out. While the Pakistani newspaper Dawn ran the headline "Good Riddance, Killer Baitullah" in celebration of the death of the man believed responsible for the assassination of former Prime Minister Benazir Bhutto, Pakistanis typically condemn similar drone strikes due to the civilian casualties they cause. In Mehsud's case, it took sixteen strikes, fourteen months and between 207 and 321 additional deaths to finally kill him. In contrast, the American government views the drone program as one of its most effective weapons against al Qaeda and the Taliban, described by CIA director Leon Panetta as "the only game in town."

The attack on Baitullah Mehsud highlights several questions about the effect of armed unmanned aerial vehicles (UAVs) on how the United States wages war. Are these strikes an effective counterterrorism tactic, even though they may cause significant civilian casualties? Furthermore, what is the effect of factors such

"Drone Wars: Armed Unmanned Aerial Vehicles," Andrew Callam, Volume XVIII, No. 3, *International Affairs Review*, Winter 2010.

as the lack of media coverage on the willingness of the United States to adopt these strikes as an effective strategy? This study seeks to address these questions and evaluate changes that armed UAVs bring to modern warfare. It will begin by offering a brief background of UAVs, their development into weaponized aircraft and their use in theater. The following section will evaluate the effect of UAVs on strategic capabilities and combat doctrine, focusing both on their use in early combat operations, counterinsurgency operations and hunter-killer missions. The next section will be devoted to problems and unanswered questions about their use, including their effect on public opinion both at home and abroad, international legal issues, and limitations. This study finds that, while armed UAVs increase the capacity of the United States military to fight insurgency and irregular warfare, their use in "hunter-killer" missions will not emerge as a dominant trend in the near future.

The Rise of the Predator: The Evolution of Drone Warfare

The idea of using a remotely-controlled, pilotless aerial vehicle emerged more than fifty years ago. However, the operational concept behind weaponized drones changed significantly over the years. The following section will provide a brief background of the evolution of weaponized UAVs, including their early use in reconnaissance missions and their expanded role by the U.S. in Afghanistan, Iraq and the Global War on Terrorism.

The use of a remotely controlled aerial vehicle as a weapon first emerged in World War II. The first remotely piloted drone used as a weapon was the German FX-1400 or "Fritz," which consisted of a 2,300 pound bomb, dropped from an airplane and steered by a pilot in the "mothership." After the war, little development occurred in drone technology and most remotely piloted vehicles were used for target practice. The U.S. military's first major expenditures on UAVs began after the Vietnam War, when the Air Force used small, long range, experimental drones called Fireflies in conducting reconnaissance over Southeast Asia. However, ensuing programs quickly ran over budget and the government deemed small propeller-powered drones too expensive to pursue on a larger scale.

The Israeli Air Force's use of their weaponized drone, the Pioneer, in the 1982 war in Lebanon reinvigorated American interest in armed UAVs. Impressed with the Pioneer, the Navy purchased several and the Reagan Administration began increasing UAV procurement and research in 1987. Powered by a 26-horsepower snowmobile engine and equipped with 16-inch guns, the Pioneer made its American debut during the Persian Gulf War. Iraqi soldiers grew to fear the ominous buzzing of the Pioneer and in one widely reported incident, a group of Republican guards became the first humans to surrender to a drone. The success of the Pioneer in Desert Storm led to the Department of Defense spending over $3 billion on UAV programs during the 1990s.

Extensive use of armed UAVs began with the Global War on Terror (GWOT), Operation Enduring Freedom (OEF), and Operation Iraqi Freedom (OIF). Up to this point, UAV missions were mostly those of intelligence, surveillance and reconnaissance purposes. In February 2001, the first Hellfire missile was test-fired from a Predator UAV. The terrorist attacks of September 11, 2001 suddenly created a new demand for Hellfire-equipped Predators to hunt down terrorists in remote areas of Afghanistan and Pakistan. The Air Force put the weaponized Predator into immediate use in OEF and hit approximately 115 targets in Afghanistan during the first year of its combat operations. The CIA also began to use Predators to target al Qaeda operatives elsewhere in the Middle East. In November 2002, a Predator was credited with killing an al Qaeda operative in Yemen, who was thought to be responsible for the USS *Cole* bombing in October 2000. The armed Predators also began patrolling Iraq as part of Operation Southern Watch. Immediately prior to OIF, Predators destroyed several Iraqi mobile radar units in preparation for the arrival of U.S. ground forces. Predators and other armed UAVs continue to carry out operations in Iraq and Afghanistan.

While the U.S. military employs a wide variety of UAVs, there are only three currently in use with offensive capabilities: the MQ-1 Predator, the MQ-1C Sky Warrior, and the MQ-9 Reaper, all three built by General Atomics. The Predator, the most commonly used drone in the American arsenal, can loiter at 25,000 feet for nearly 40 hours, and is equipped with two Hellfire missiles and two cameras—one infrared and one regular—that can read a license plate from two miles up. The Army's Sky Warrior is a slightly larger version of the Predator that can fly slightly higher, loiter for a shorter amount of time, and carry two more missiles than the Predator. The Reaper, also known as the Predator B, is the largest and most powerful of the three drone models. The Reaper can fly at twice the altitude and speed of the Predator and can carry eight Hellfire missiles or four missiles and two laser-guided bombs. It also carries an improved camera and software package that can "recognize and categorize humans and human-made objects," such as improvised explosive devices. Although the Defense Department's 2011 budget doubles spending on the Reaper, the Predator will remain the primary UAV in use.

The operational use of weaponized UAVs can be divided into two broad categories; direct support of military operation and hunter-killer missions. As mentioned above, the military first utilized UAVs in the early operations of OEF and OIF as both a weapon and surveillance tool and they proved particularly useful in identifying, locating and eliminating targets. In describing the utility of UAVs in OEF, CENTCOM commander General Tommy Franks said: "The Predator is my most capable sensor in hunting down and killing al Qaeda and Taliban leadership and is proving critical to our fight." By 2007, the military began utilizing drones in counterinsurgency operations in Iraq and demand for drones skyrocketed. Drones continue to serve in supporting operations to American forces in Afghanistan and Iraq.

In contrast, the CIA's drone program in the tribal areas of Pakistan utilizes weaponized UAVs primarily in hunter-killer missions. This program, begun under the George W. Bush Administration as part of the GWOT, uses drones primarily in "search and destroy" missions aimed at terrorism suspects and Taliban leadership in Pakistan. One important difference between the two programs is that while the military program operates exclusively in recognized combat zones, the CIA program flies drones over civilian areas as well. The CIA conducts these strikes with the reluctant and implicit support of the Pakistani government, which has publicly condemned the attacks, but continues to allow the CIA to base the drones in its territory. According to a former White House counterterrorism official, the CIA has multiple drones constantly scouting the tribal areas of Pakistan for targets.

The Obama Administration has dramatically increased the number of CIA drone attacks since taking office. Under President Bush, the CIA carried out only 2 strikes in 2006 and 3 in 2007. In July 2008, Bush increased the number of drone strikes, totaling 34 attacks in 2008. Most of the key CIA personnel from the Bush Administration's drone program remain, but the Obama Administration has far outpaced its predecessor in the frequency of drone strikes. By October 19th, 2009, the CIA had conducted 41 strikes under President Obama, compared with the same number over three years under former President Bush. CIA drone strikes under the Obama Administration show no signs of abating. The agency has conducted 11 strikes in Pakistan during the first month of 2010.

The Effect of Armed UAVs on Military Capabilities

The development of UAVs' offensive capabilities has led to three broad operational concepts regarding the use of UAVs in combat. These concepts include the use of UAVs to: 1) suppress enemy air defense, 2) support counterinsurgency operations, and 3) find and eliminate enemy targets. The following section will discuss how the U.S. military and CIA employ UAVs and the effect of their use on operational capabilities.

The use of UAVs to suppress enemy air defenses first emerged in the first months of OIF. As previously mentioned, the Air Force attempted to use Predators to destroy Iraqi defense installations. However, the Predator proved too slow and vulnerable for Iraqi MIGs, which quickly shot down several Predators. As a result, UAV use in the suppression of enemy air defenses is limited in practice. This may change in the future as the Department of Defense foresees UAVs eventually fulfilling strike missions in early combat operations as discussed in the Unmanned Aircraft Systems Roadmap, 2005–2030.

UAVs also proved useful during counterinsurgency operations in Iraq. The stabilization of Sadr City in 2008 is a dramatic example of the utility of drones in counterinsurgency warfare. In this instance, U.S. colonels on the ground could directly control armed drones hovering over the streets of Baghdad. This was the first time drones were used at the brigade level. For example, after militants fired a rocket at an American position, an American battalion would deploy a Predator drone to survey the area as insurgents set up their next shot, then destroy the enemy's mortar positions. The Predator could also loiter above the battle area, relaying the insurgents' patterns and tactics to commanders on the ground. In one instance, a Predator drone hovered above a house that was a suspected weapons cache, waited for civilians to leave, and then destroyed the building with a Hellfire missile. The Predator granted the battalion persistent surveillance and strike capabilities, which proved crucial in stabilizing Sadr City.

In counterinsurgency warfare, the main benefit of the armed drone is an increased ability to "find, fix and finish" enemy combatants, while minimizing civilian casualties. Traditionally, aerial surveillance vehicles would observe a suspected target and radio the coordinates to an operations center, where personnel would consult maps and senior officers in an attempt to identify civilian structures. Following the consultation, the operations center would relay instructions to an airborne craft. In Operation Desert Storm, this process (also know as the "kill chain" or "sensor-to shooter-cycle") could take up to three days, by which time the targets could have left the target building or civilians could have entered it. When armed drones are used, the kill chain is only one link long and the process takes less than 5 minutes. Additionally, as P.W. Singer, author of *Wired for War*, notes, using an unmanned drone allows the pilot to take more risks with his craft, such as flying lower and loitering longer, thus leading to a more accurate strike. The drones therefore allow commanders to avoid killing noncombatants during their strikes, a crucial element in counterinsurgency warfare.

In contrast, the CIA primarily utilizes its Predator drones in the third type of operation: hunter-killer missions. These operations can extend U.S. offensive capabilities into areas in which the United States has little or no access. The Predator allows the CIA to scout the skies of the lawless and inaccessible tribal regions of Pakistan and eliminate terrorism suspects without utilizing ground troops. Some have viewed this development as a costless way to fight terrorism and extend American offensive and deterrent capabilities. For example, the new capabilities of the CIA's drone program have shaped the debate over U.S. strategy in Afghanistan. In an influential editorial, conservative pundit George Will made the case for an American withdrawal from Afghanistan, arguing that "America should do only what can be done from offshore, using intelligence drones, cruise missiles, airstrikes and small, potent Special Forces unites, concentrating on the porous 1,500-mile border with Pakistan." Vice President Joe Biden had also reportedly ascribed to this view regarding strategy in Afghanistan. What began as a tactic to combat terrorism has gained credence as a strategy to extend American influence without committing troops.

There is also evidence that the persistent surveillance and attack capabilities of drones serve as a deterrent to potential combatants and sow paranoia and distrust among terrorists groups. Warfare theorists believe that the constant surveillance and persistent attack capabilities have a striking effect on the enemy's behavior. As a drone pilot in Iraq described it: "Anti-Iraqi forces know we are out there. They know they are constantly being watched. The fear of being caught in the act keeps a lot of would-be insurgents out of the fight." Journalist David Rohde, who spent seven months imprisoned by the Taliban, described the paranoia among his captors following a drone strike: "They believed that a network of local informants guided the missiles. Innocent civilians were rounded up, accused of working as American spies and then executed." Some Pakistanis in FATA have even stopped drinking Lipton tea because they believe the CIA puts homing beacons for the drones in the tea bags. This demonstrates the psychological effect weaponized drones can have on both existing and potential enemy combatants.

Limitations, Costs and Unanswered Questions

Although the military and CIA have integrated armed UAVs into a variety of operations, their use is still limited by their vulnerability to minimal air defenses. While the Predators succeeded in striking down some Iraqi radar units during OIF, they quickly became a target for Iraqi air defenses. The Iraqi Air Force shot down three Predators with relative ease. This vulnerability to basic air defenses and limited air-to-air defensive capabilities invalidated the concept of using UAVs in missions to suppress enemy air defenses.

The drones' vulnerability to air defenses also has implications for using UAVs to extend American strategic capabilities. These limitations restrict UAV use to missions in regions where air defense threats have been eliminated. Even in the tribal regions of Pakistan, where there are virtually no air defenses, members of the Taliban claimed to have shot down several CIA drones over South Waziristan. Even when not facing enemy fire, the Predator crashes due to mechanical error 43 times per 100,000 flying hours, whereas typical manned aircraft crash 2 per 100,000 hours. The high attrition rate of UAVs in the face of enemy fire makes it unlikely that they will soon serve as a replacement for manned aircraft.

The lack of military presence on the ground also limits the capability of drones to assist in acquiring critical intelligence. In the urban counterinsurgency operations of Iraq, UAVs would use their persistent surveillance capabilities to observe combatants, then either eliminate or send in ground troops to arrest the combatant. The combatant might then go on to provide U.S. forces with valuable intelligence. In contrast, the use of UAVs in hunter-killer operations in the remote regions of Pakistan, where there are no ground forces, only eliminates the target. As Daniel Byman of Georgetown University argues, "it's almost always better to arrest terrorists than to kill them. You get intelligence then. Dead men tell no tales." Hunter-killer operations can only eliminate the target and thus forfeit potential intelligence that could be gained through capture.

The lack of multiple intelligence sources also inhibits the ability of drones to accurately identify targets. Local informants are notoriously unreliable and can exploit the attacks for personal gain by pointing drone attacks towards personal rivals. Additionally, while the Predator's camera can provide remarkably clear images, it can be difficult for drone pilots to accurately identify individuals when staring at them directly from above. For example, just months after the September 11th attacks, a Predator pilot spotted a tall man in flowing white robes walking near the eastern border of Afghanistan. Intelligence officials incorrectly believed the man to be Osama bin Laden and fired the Predator's missile, killing the innocent villager and his two companions. Without a persistent ground presence, drones must act with incomplete intelligence and may cause civilian casualties.

Civilian deaths caused by the CIA's drone program are one of the main criticisms of using drones exclusively in hunter-killer missions. Since 2006, 82 drone attacks in Pakistan have killed between 750 and 1,000 people, including between 250 and 320 civilians, equivalent to roughly 1 civilian death for every 3 militants killed. Some experts claim that the collateral damage of these attacks creates more militants than they eliminate. "The drone war has created a siege mentality among Pakistani civilians," says Andrew Exum and David Kilcullen of the Center for New American Security. "While violent extremists may be unpopular, for a frightened population they seem less ominous than a faceless enemy that wages war from afar and often kills more civilians than militants." If the civilian deaths caused by drone attacks are indeed solidifying the popular support of Islamic militants, the drone program may prevent success in northwest Pakistan.

Some argue that the use of such advanced technology will encourage further acts of terrorism. The Taliban carried out its March 2009 attack on the Lahore police academy "in retaliation for the continued drone strikes." Hakimullah Mehsud, Baitullah Mehsud's successor as leader of the Pakistani Taliban, said the Taliban "will continue to launch suicide attacks until U.S. drone attacks are stopped." Like many innovations in military technologies throughout history, the enemy and local civilians perceive them as evil. Regarding Israel's operations in Lebanon, a Lebanese man described the impression of Israel's use of UAVs as that "of an evil, brutal enemy that will use any means to accomplish its goals." In some regions, Pakistani mothers use the Predator attacks as a type of boogey-man—"Obey or the 'buzz' will come after you" —and in 2007, a popular song in Pakistan accused America of "killing people like insects." Paradoxically, attacks that are aimed at eliminating terrorists may in some cases encourage terrorism.

Others argue that the drone attacks are the United States' most effective weapon against terrorism. Only a few of the recent terrorism plots against the United States can be traced back to Pakistan and al Qaeda seems to be more concerned with self-preservation than carrying out attacks since the expansion of the drone program. Even their effect on the Pakistani population is questionable. In a survey conducted in FATA, a thin majority thought that the drone attacks were mostly accurate and did not increase anti-American sentiments. This conflicting evidence makes the net effect of drone attacks difficult to judge.

It is also unclear whether the CIA's Predator program in Pakistan, which is not a recognized war zone, falls in line with international law. Before deploying the weaponized Predator drone, the U.S. government deemed armed UAVs fully compliant with the Intermediate range Nuclear Forces Treaty and other international agreements. However, the U.S. government has yet to conduct a review that ensures that the targeted killings are in accordance with international law. Many lawyers conclude that the attacks meet the basic test to target civilian terror suspects abroad, but certain questions remain. P.W. Singer, "in the hundreds of interviews" he conducted for his book *Wired for War*, found no references to international law. He also found that no one could answer who in the chain of command would be prosecuted if mistakes were made. Columbia University Law Professor Matthew Waxman notes that there is no consensus on the principal of proportionality in international law, namely how to balance the equation of military gains with civilian casualties. Recently, a United Nations human rights investigator stated that "the United States must demonstrate that it is not randomly killing people in violation of international law through its use of drones." As the drone program continues to cause civilian casualties, it will likely come under greater scrutiny regarding its compliance with international law.

The lack of attention paid to the legal issues and civilian casualties surrounding the CIA's drone program underlies the general apathy of the American public towards drone warfare. This suggests that using drones instead of humans can lead to the perception of a "costless war." The first reason for this is that these strikes occur away from American eyes. Journalists typically cannot enter areas where the drone strikes occur and, in the case of Baitullah Mehsud, the Taliban disrupted phone lines and set up defenses to prevent word of Mehsud's death from leaking out. Very few videos or photographs of the drone strikes are available to the public, which isolates Americans from the damage these strikes can cause.

The second and more crucial reason for the perception of a "costless war" is the fact that waging a war with drones quite literally comes at no human costs to the United States. By their very nature, UAVs offer two advantages over manned aircraft: they are cheaper and eliminate the risk of a pilot's life. The potential drawback of this is that, without men and women coming home in coffins, the American public is less likely to object to war and, in the words of *New York Times* columnist Roger Cohen, "going to war can become hard to distinguish from going to work." The "costless war" erodes the political checks and accountability that are characteristic of waging war in a democratic society. Taking this argument to its logical extreme, removing costs from war could lead to an increased willingness to use force, essentially invalidating the premise of the democratic peace theory.

The Future of Drone Warfare

It is clear that the United States military sees drone warfare as the wave of the future. The Department of Defense continues to increase its budget for unmanned systems and will purchase 24 additional Reapers and 36 additional Sky Warriors in fiscal year 2010. The UAV fleet will also continue to modernize. By the end of 2010, the Air Force's Boeing X-45 Unmanned Combat Aerial Vehicle (UCAV) will make its first flight and the Navy's X-47 UCAV will soon follow. UCAVs differ from armed UAVs in that UCAVs can perform similar tasks as modern manned fighter aircraft, namely defending themselves against enemy aircraft and flying at fast enough speeds to avoid surface-to-air defenses. While weaponized UAVs are currently more suitable to low-intensity conflicts like those in Iraq and Afghanistan, UCAVs will be able to participate in high- and medium-intensity conflict and could be used to suppress enemy air defenses in advance of a ground mission. Unmanned blimps, bombers, attack helicopters and surveillance and detection UAVs that resemble grasshoppers, flies, bees and spiders are all in the military's playbook. The Defense Department's 2011 budget request plans to double the production of unmanned aircraft.

As current trends demonstrate, weaponized UAVs will increase the capability to fight low-intensity and insurgency warfare. Armed UAVs provide troops fighting in counterinsurgency operations with several advantages. First, they provide both the surveillance and attack capabilities to carry out precise counterterrorism missions without actually deploying troops to the specific area.

Removing a pilot's life from the equation also allows UAVs to provide more accurate intelligence in pursuit of avoiding civilian casualties. Armed UAVs also shorten the kill chain to just one link, allowing ground commanders to make snap decisions and exert more control over the battle space.

Despite the advantages in counterinsurgency operations, UAVs are unlikely to change the fundamental nature of American warfare in the near future. As Manjeet Singh Pardesi argues, UAVs are not a "disruptive technology as there will always be missions that will require the manned aircraft." Current UAV systems are simply too vulnerable to carry out missions independently and can only effectively operate as a compliment to U.S. ground forces in areas in which air defense systems have been largely eliminated. Even in this case, the attrition rate is very high. UAV missions will continue to be limited to the "dull, dirty and dangerous" tasks, until they develop capabilities comparable to manned aircraft. Because ground troops are needed, there is no indication of an increased willingness to engage in conflict. As long as humans carry out the primary missions of warfare, there will continue to be political costs to engaging in conflict.

The CIA's drone program in Pakistan is a unique and important exception to many of the limitations governing UAVs. A primary benefit of using UAVs in these combat operations is the ability to limit civilian casualties, yet collateral damage is a major problem in using drones in "hunter-killer" missions. Whereas most UAVs operate in areas with a ground presence, CIA drones go where American troops cannot and can operate nearly autonomously. The CIA's program in Pakistan therefore contradicts many of the trends in weaponized UAV warfare.

However, the CIA's drone program can function only in very specific circumstances and is unlikely to represent a lasting trend in warfare. Few regions in the world are as remote as northwest Pakistan and the drone program capitalizes on the very distinctive characteristics of the region. The barriers to using drones in "hunter-killer" missions in other parts of the world including increased media coverage, violations of international law, and the threat of the most basic air defenses, makes the drone program in most other countries impractical. Further, there is no end-game to using a hunter-killer strategy. Using drones without a manned ground presence to truly neutralize the enemy will lead to short-term gains but is not a substitute for a long-term strategy.

The effect that UAVs will have on future warfare will depend largely on technological capabilities of the next generation of drones. In the near future, armed drones will continue to serve as a complement to manned systems, rather than a replacement. While the circumstances in northwest Pakistan are unique, the questions surrounding the CIA's drone program in Pakistan raise important issues regarding how drone use should be governed in the future. As the capabilities of robotic systems continue to improve at a rapid rate, policymakers should begin answering these questions now in order to prevent the progress of technology from surpassing the moral and legal considerations governing their use.

To answer these questions, policymakers must first launch a review of international legal implications of the CIA's drone program. As Jane Mayer of *The New Yorker* pointed out in her groundbreaking article on the drone program, the Predator strikes into Pakistan can easily be considered assassinations. While the United States policy officially abandoned assassinations during the Ford Administration, the legal justification of the drone program has gone largely unquestioned by the American public. If the United States seeks to be a cooperative member of the international community, it must be able to justify the drone program according to international legal standards.

The issue that has received far more attention than the legal implications, however, has been the civilian deaths caused by the drone program in Pakistan. While many suspect that the strikes do more harm than good, the fact remains that little evidence exists to support any argument. The intelligence community must therefore conduct a thorough study of the effect of these drone strikes on the population in Pakistan. This study must be able to accurately measure the amount of collateral damage caused per successful strike. The study must also seek to answer whether or not the strikes radicalize the Pakistani population. If the strikes in actuality undermine the stability of the Pakistani state, the CIA program must be either cancelled or its standards reevaluated.

While drones have improved the capabilities of the U.S. military, unmanned systems will never replace humans on the battlefield. Particularly in counterinsurgency warfare, UAVs can help protect soldiers and minimize civilian casualties, but the human element is still crucial to the success of low intensity conflict. The capabilities of UAVs must never be mistaken for a strategy or a way to wage a "costless war." Viewing technological improvements as such will only lead to a militarization of foreign policy and unnecessary conflicts. Policymakers must therefore proceed cautiously when employing these technologies in the field and develop new standards for their use. Unmanned systems may lead to a safer type of warfare for U.S. soldiers, but they will be unable to eliminate the inherent brutality of war.

We Will Regret Our Use of Drones

Doyle McManus

Doyle McManus is an American journalist and columnist who appears often on Public Broadcasting Service's Washington Week.

The drone has become America's counter-terrorism weapon of choice. But does drone warfare really further U.S. goals abroad?

To wartime strategists under both George W. Bush and Barack Obama, the new weapon, like many innovations in the history of military technology, seemed at first like a silver bullet.

Drones with lethal missiles could hover for hours over potential targets, waiting for the moment to strike. They could kill suspected terrorists with relative precision, though not, as the CIA claimed in 2011, without any civilian casualties. Best of all, drones didn't endanger American lives; the pilots were safe and snug in Djibouti or Nevada.

In an almost-invisible campaign that started modestly under Bush and expanded dramatically under Obama, the U.S. has launched more than 1,600 drone strikes in Afghanistan, Iraq, Pakistan, Yemen, Somalia, Libya and even, in one case, in the Philippines, according to Micah Zenko of the Council on Foreign Relations.

But consider how those drone strikes appear if you are an ordinary civilian in, say, northwestern Pakistan. You know you are in constant danger; a missile may strike your home at any time without warning. It's not clear who's shooting; the war and its combatants are officially secret. It's not clear how you can avoid becoming a target; members of Al Qaeda are fair game, of course, but what are their neighbors and cousins and grocery suppliers to do? And if something goes awry, there's no one to complain to; the

"The Drone Warfare Drawbacks," Doyle McManus, *Los Angeles Times*, July 5, 2014. Reprinted by permission.

CIA doesn't have a customer service desk, and the government of Pakistan claims (falsely, in most cases) that it has no control over foreign missile strikes.

Drone strikes may be an efficient way to kill terrorists, but they're no way to make friends.

That's one of the messages of a stinging new report issued recently by a panel of experts convened by Washington's independent Stimson Center, a thoroughly establishment group of former officials from both Democratic and Republican administrations. Blue-ribbon commissions in Washington often pull their punches; this one, chaired by retired Army Gen. John P. Abizaid and former Pentagon official Rosa Brooks, didn't. Among its highlights:

Just because drone wars have succeeded in killing terrorists doesn't mean they're working. "The Obama administration's heavy reliance on targeted killings as a pillar of U.S. counter-terrorism strategy rests on questionable assumptions and risks increasing instability," the report warns. After a decade of drone strikes, it notes, we face more Islamic extremists, not fewer.

The widespread use of drones has created a backlash around the world, and not only in remote villages in Pakistan or Yemen. The report quotes retired Gen. Stanley McChrystal, the former U.S. commander in Afghanistan, warning that the tactic creates resentment "much greater than the average American appreciates."

Reliance on drones for "targeted killing" has allowed the CIA and Pentagon to obscure exactly whom we are fighting. About the only thing the Obama administration has said on the subject is that it has aimed the drone program at "Al Qaeda and associated forces." But, as the report notes, while U.S. targeters may exercise great care in their decisions, the drone attacks still look perilously like "a secret war, governed by secret law."

Our drone policy could come back to haunt us once the U.S. loses its current near-monopoly in drone technology. China and Iran are already working on military drones, and Russia is unlikely to be far behind. If Vladimir Putin decided to use drones against anti-Russian militants in Ukraine, the report notes, "Russia could simply repeat the words used by U.S. officials defending U.S. targeted killings, asserting that it could not provide any evidence without disclosing sources and methods."

The ease of using drones makes them seductively tempting to deploy. "The increasing use of lethal drones may create a slippery slope leading to continual or wider wars," the panel warned. "[Drones] may lower the bar to enter a conflict, without increasing the likelihood of a satisfactory outcome." Obama has assiduously avoided one slippery slope, the one that leads to putting U.S. troops on the ground, but he's presided over the creation of another.

Given all those issues, the report notes, it might be a good moment for a pause in the drone wars. But don't hold your breath waiting for that to happen.

Many of the Stimson Center's findings "resonate with the administration's current policy," National Security Council spokeswoman Caitlin Hayden told me last week. "As the president said last month at West Point, the United States 'must be more transparent about both the basis of our counter-terrorism actions and the manner in which they are carried out.'"

But that doesn't mean the administration plans to abandon drone warfare. It has already said it may soon use the missiles on a new battlefield against the Islamic State of Iraq and Syria, which has shortened its name to Islamic State.

The Stimson Center report gives the administration a smart list of policy proposals: a systematic review of drones' costs and benefits; a commission on targeting, to show that we're very careful about whom we kill; and an effort to establish international norms, so when Russia and Iran get drones some basic rules are in place.

I'll add one more: The administration should make public its enemies list. It's past time that the U.S. disclosed a list of organizations that qualify as "Al Qaeda associates," and thus as legitimate targets for U.S. attack. If secrecy is necessary in some cases, keep those secret. But even a partial list would be better than we have now: a secret war governed by secret law.

How Effective Are Drones in Securing Our Borders?

Overview: Understanding Our Increasingly Militarized Borders

Tom Barry

Tom Barry is a senior policy analyst at the Center for International Policy, where he directs the TransBorder Project. Barry specializes in immigration policy, homeland security, border security, and the outsourcing of national security.

The Department of Homeland Security (DHS) says it is the "leading edge" of drone deployment in the United States. Since 2005, DHS has been purchasing Predator drones—officially called unmanned aerial systems (UAS)—to "secure the border," yet these unarmed Predator drones are also steadily creeping into local law enforcement, international drug-interdiction and national security missions—including across the border into the heart of Mexico.

DHS will likely double its drone contingent to two dozen unmanned UAS produced by General Atomics as part of the border security component of any immigration reform. The prominence of border security in immigration reform can't be missed. The leading reform proposal, offered by eight US senators, is the Border Security, Economic Opportunity, and Immigration Modernization Act of 2013—which proposes to spend $6.5 billion in additional "border security" measures, mostly high-tech surveillance by drones and ground surveillance systems.

Most of the concern about the domestic deployment of drones by DHS has focused on the crossover to law-enforcement missions that threaten privacy and civil rights, and that, without more regulations in place, the program will accelerate the transition to what critics call a "surveillance society." Also alarming is the mission creep of border drones, managed by the DHS' Customs

"Drones Over the Homeland: From Border Security to National Security," Tom Barry, Truthout, May 19, 2013. Reprinted by permission.

and Border Protection (CPB) agency with increasing interface between border drones, international drug interdiction operations and other military-directed national security missions.

The prevalence of military jargon used by US Customs and Border (CBP) officials - such as "defense in depth" and "situational awareness"—points to at least a rhetorical overlapping of border control and military strategy. Another sign of the increasing coincidence between CBP/Office of Airforce and Marine (OAM) drone program and the military is that the commanders and deputies of OAM are retired military officers. Both Major General Michael Kostelnik and his successor Major General Randolph Alles, retired from US Marines, were highly placed military commanders involved in drone development and procurement.

Kostelnik has been involved in the development of the Predator by General Atomics since the mid-1990s and was an early proponent of providing Air Force funding to weaponize the Predator. As commander of the Marine Corps Warfighting Laboratory, Alles was a leading proponent of having each military branch work with military contractors to develop their own drone breeds, including near replicas of the Predator manufactured for the Army by General Atomics.

In promoting—and justifying—the DHS drone program, Kostelnik has routinely alluded to the national security potential of drones slated for border security duty. On several occasions Kostelnik has pointed to the seamless interoperability with Department of Defense (DOD) Unmanned Aerial Vehicle (UAV) forces. At a moment's notice, Kostelnik said, that OAM (Office of Airforce and Marine) could be "CHOP'ed"—meaning undergo a Change in Operational Command from DHS to DOD.

DHS has not released operational data about CBP (Customs and Border Protection)/OAM drone operations. Therefore, the extent of the participation of DHS drones in domestic and international operations is unknown. But statements by CBP officials and media reports from the Caribbean point to a rapidly expanding participation of DHS Guardian UAVs in drug-interdiction and other unspecified operations as far south as Panama. CBP states that OAM "routinely provides air and marine support to other federal, state and local law enforcement agencies" and "works with the US military in joint international antismuggling operations and in support of National Security Special Events [such as the Olympics]."

According to Kostelnik, CBP planned a "Spring 2011 deployment of the Guardian to a Central American country in association with Joint Interagency Task Force South (JIATF-South) based at the naval station in Key West, Florida." JIATF-South is a subordinate command to the United States Southern Command (USSOUTHCOM), whose geographical purview includes the Caribbean, Central America and South America. In mid-2012, CBP/OAM participated in a JIATF-South collaborative venture called "Operation Caribbean Focus" that involved flight over the Caribbean Sea and nations in the region—with the Dominican Republic acting as the regional host for the Guardian operations, which CBP/OAM considers a "prototype for future transit zone UAS (drone) deployments."

CBP has been secretly deploying Predators into Mexican territory. In its description of the OAM operations, CBP states, "OAM works in collaboration with the Government of Mexico in addressing border security issues." But it has never publicly specified the form and the objectives of this collaboration. Nor has it publicly acknowledged that its Predator drones have entered Mexican territory.

As part of the US global drug war and as an extension of border security, the US Northern Command acknowledged that the military was deploying—with the approval of the Mexican government—the $38 million Global Hawk drone into Mexico as part of the joint US-Mexico attempt to suppress the Mexican drug cartels.

CBP says that OAM drones have not been deployed within Mexico, but notes that "OAM works in collaboration with the Government of Mexico in addressing border security issues, "without specifying the form and objectives of this collaboration." As part of the US global drug war and as an extension of border security, unarmed drones are also crossing the border into Mexico. The US Northern Command has acknowledged that the US military does fly a $38-million Global Hawk drone into Mexico to assist Mexico's war against the drug cartels.

An April 28 *Washington Post* article by Dana Priest raises new questions and concerns about the increasing mission creep of homeland drones into foreign missions involving the U.S. military, CIA and Drug Enforcement Administration (DEA).

President Felipe Calderón began requesting US drone flights into Mexico on targeted killings missions soon after he became president in December 2006. However, it wasn't until the July 2009 killing of a US Border Patrol agent by suspected Mexican drug smugglers that the US government began deploying unarmed Predator drones.

According to *Washington Post* reporter Priest, "[H]ours after Mexican smugglers shot and killed a U.S. Border Patrol agent while trying to steal his night-vision goggles, U.S. authorities were given permission to fly an unarmed Predator drone into Mexican airspace to hunt for suspects. Intelligence from the flights was passed to the Mexican army. Within 12 hours, the army brought back more information, according to two U.S. officials involved in the operation. Eventually, four suspects were captured. Three pleaded guilty, one is awaiting trial and a fifth remains at large."

"That first flight dispelled Mexican fears that U.S. authorities would try to take control of drone operations," noted the Washington Post article, "An agreement was reached that would temporarily give operational control to Mexican authorities during such flights. U.S. pilots sitting in the states would control the planes remotely, but a Mexican military or federal police commander would be able to direct the pilot within the boundaries of a Mexico-designated grid. By late 2010, drones were flying deeper into Mexico to spy on the cartels ..."

CBP has never stated for the public record that its Predators are being deployed over Mexican territory. In an attempt to clarify the nature and extent of Predator surveillance in Mexico, Truthout asked CBP to confirm that OAM drones stationed along the border were indeed being deployed into Mexico and whether CBP maintained operational control of these missions or whether CBP drones were piloted by nonagency personnel from the military or intelligence sector.

CBP officials declined to speak for attribution. Instead, a CBP official responded anonymously and ambiguously, stating:

> As part of the bilateral security cooperation, the Government of Mexico has asked the US government— in certain instances —for the support of unmanned aircraft to gather specific intelligence, particularly along the border region, in order to achieve concrete security goals. When such operations take place, Mexican authorities have the operational authorization, oversight and supervision.
>
> In 2009, the United States requested approval from the Mexican government to fly in Mexican airspace to support law enforcement officers assigned to search and apprehend Agent Rosas' murder suspects who fled into Mexico.
>
> During the current administration, the emphasis on the collaboration of information sharing has assisted in the fight of criminal organizations that affects populations on both sides of the border. Within this framework, information and greater intelligence gathering capabilities have been made available to both governments, to include support of unmanned aircraft.

Left hanging was the question about the role of DOD and the intelligence sector in piloting CBP drones and in analyzing the resulting surveillance data. It also remains unclear whether the Mexican government interacts directly with DHS and CBP/OAM or, in making its requests for drone surveillance, it bypasses DHS entirely.

Increased border security funding and more drones are a core part of all immigration reform proposals being introduced in

Congress. However, because of the secrecy and lack of transparency and accountability that is systemic in the DHS border agencies, it is likely neither the Congress nor the US public understands that increasing the number of border security Predators also likely increases the foreign deployment of these drones in nonborder missions over foreign nations and international waters.

Communities, state legislatures and even some congressional members are proceeding to enact legislation and revise ordinances to decriminalize or legalize the consumption of drugs, especially marijuana, targeted by the federal government's drug war of more than four decades. At the same time, DHS has been escalating its contributions to the domestic and international drug war—in the name of both homeland security and national security. Drug seizures on the border and drug interdiction over coastal and neighboring waters are certainly the top operative priorities of OAM. Enlisting its Guardian drones in SOUTHCOM's drug interdiction efforts underscores the increasing emphasis within the entire CBP on counter-narcotic operations.

CBP is a DHS agency that is almost exclusively focused on tactics. While CBP, as the umbrella agency, the Office of the Border Patrol and OAM all have strategic plans, these plans are marked by their rigid military frameworks, their startling absence of serious strategic thinking and the diffuse distinctions between strategic goals and tactics. As a result of the border security buildup, south-north drug flows (particularly cocaine and more high-value drugs) have shifted back to marine smuggling, mainly through the Caribbean, but also through the Gulf of Mexico and the Pacific.

Rather than reevaluating drug prohibition and drug control frameworks for border policy, CBP/OAM has rationalized the procurement of more UAVs on the shifts in the geographical arenas of the drug war—albeit couching the tactical changes in the new drug war language of "transnational criminal organizations" and "narcoterrorism." The overriding framework for CBP/OAM operations is evolving from border security and homeland security to national security, as recent CBP presentations about its Guardian deployments illustrate.

Shortly before retiring after seven years as OAM's first chief, Major Gen. Kostelnik told a gathering of military contractors: "CPB's UAS Deployment Vision strengthens the National Security Response Capability." He may well be right, but the US public and Congress need to know if DHS plans to institute guidelines and limits that regulate the extent of DHS operational collaboration with DOD and the CIA.

Drones Are a Cheaper and More Efficient Means of Patrolling Borders

Trahern Jones

Trahern Jones was a journalism fellow in the Walter Cronkite School of Journalism and Mass Communication's Two Borders Project.

CORPUS CHRISTI, Texas — Despite critical reports saying that the use of drones to patrol the nation's borders is inefficient and costly, the leading Congressional proposal for immigration reform would drastically expand their use.

In fact, the compromise bill would have U.S. Customs and Border Protection, which currently has a fleet of 10 Predator drones, using the unmanned aircraft to patrol the southern border with Mexico 24 hours a day, seven days a week.

An expanded drone program is also sure to draw the ire of privacy advocates who already worry that increasing use of unmanned aircraft will result in intrusive surveillance of U.S. citizens.

The proposal for around-the-clock drone use flies in the face of recent reports from the Government Accountability Office and the Office of the Inspector General.

In a 2012 report, the OIG estimated that the agency only used its current Predator fleet about 40 percent of the time it had projected for use of the crafts. The same report criticized CBP for failing "to obtain reimbursement for missions flown on stakeholders' behalf," such as U.S. Border Patrol, local law enforcement or emergency organizations, like FEMA.

Criticism of the program also came in a 2012 GAO report that said drone program staff frequently had to be relocated from other regions to support Predator operations on the southwestern border. In spite of such measures, the report noted that air support requests were more often left unfulfilled in this high-priority region when compared to lower-priority areas like the Canadian border.

Initiated in 2005 at a cost of nearly $18 million for each of the 10 drones and their support systems, the use of unmanned aircraft is a relatively new tool for the Custom and Border Protection's Office of Air and Marine.

While agency officials say that the program is useful in border surveillance, Predator aircraft cannot be launched on a 24/7 basis due to weather conditions and safety regulations.

Unmanned aerial vehicles are usually restricted to regions and altitudes where other aircraft do not share the same airspace in order to prevent mid-air collisions. That's why CBP's Predator fleet almost always flies at night, further limiting potential operational hours.

During an April visit to the National Air Security Operations Center in Corpus Christi, Texas, which controls Predator flights over the Rio Grande, Cronkite student reporters observed that high winds deterred launches for four days.

A pilot for the program, who requested to be unnamed for security reasons, described some of the challenges the agency has had in learning the new systems.

"We're bringing our people up and getting more experience," he said. "The technology changes; they can change the software. They can give us new payloads. Things come pretty fast in the unmanned aircraft world as opposed to the manned aviation world."

The drones fly for an average of seven to nine hours a mission, often covering many miles of uninhabited deserts, rivers and forests. CBP's Predator aircraft are equipped with high-tech cameras and communications equipment to coordinate with Border Patrol and first responder agencies on the ground. Unlike the Predator program used in overseas military missions, CBP's fleet does not carry weapons payloads.

The aircraft often provide useful information for agents in complex situations or difficult-to-reach areas, according to Hector

Black, border patrol associate Chief, and the agency's liaison with CBP's Office of Air and Marine at the Corpus Christi Predator Operations Center.

"When we come across something, we'll contact the guys on the ground," Black said in a phone interview. "Rather than sending agents in their vehicle, where it may take an hour and a half or two hours to get out and look at these areas, we can cover it in five or ten minutes with this aircraft."

The camera equipment aboard CBP Predators is sophisticated enough, according to Black, that even from an altitude of many thousands of feet, "you can actually zoom in and get street names."

While the same camera equipment can be found on the agency's manned aircraft, the Predator's longer flying time allows for increased surveillance and more immediate responsiveness to situations on the ground, according to CBP officials.

In attempting to measure the successes or failures of the program, Black cautioned that metrics like apprehensions, seizures or flight hours might not be appropriate. Predator missions are often used for intelligence-gathering purposes, alongside interceptions of illegal crossings.

A more subtle measure of drones' effectiveness is how they impact smuggling patterns in areas they patrol, Black said.

"First we'll see a spike in apprehensions in those zones, and then the spikes will start to show a direct downward trend," he noted.

Not everyone is convinced of their effectiveness, however. The perceived shortfalls noted by the GAO and OIG represent a systemic problem, according to Ed Herlik, a researcher with Market Info Group, an aviation and defense analysis firm.

"They already don't fly their Predators much at all," Herlik said in a phone interview. "We ran the numbers. Part of the time there are no Predators in the air anywhere in the nation and most of the time there might be one."

"Now, of course they can launch two or three or five if they want to," he added, "but they almost never do, just by running the averages from what they report from flight times."

The reason for the program's existence in the first place may have had more to do with the politics of border security than actual need, according to Herlik.

"The Predators were forced on them" he said.

Herlik explained that such systems were adapted from their wartime purposes in Iraq and Afghanistan for domestic use.

"Congress wanted Predators over the border, therefore it happened," Herlik said. "The fact that they're not tremendously useful is not helpful."

Congressman Henry Cuellar, D-Tex, the co-chair of the House of Representatives Unmanned Systems Caucus, countered that CBP's drone program is a useful tool to be explored further.

"You need technology, whether it's cameras, sensors or unmanned aerial vehicles, for example," Cuellar said in a phone interview. "We need the right mixture of personnel and technology to secure the border."

Cuellar said the use of technology on the border is "evolving."

As co-chair of Congress's Unmanned Systems Caucus, Cuellar came under fire in 2012 when an investigation by Hearst Newspapers and the Center for Responsive Politics revealed that caucus members had received almost $8 million in campaign contributions from unmanned aircraft manufacturers and lobbying groups. Cuellar himself received $10,000 in contributions from General Atomics, the California-based company that produced CBP's Predator fleet.

When questioned about such contributions, he emphasized that, like most members of Congress, he gets donations from a variety of interest groups with conflicting goals.

"I receive campaign contributions from those companies that produce aircraft, that produce technology—in this case, unmanned aerial vehicles—just like I've received money from media PACs," Cuellar said. "They never ask me if their contribution affects me."

CBP's Predator fleet has also been criticized for its potential impact on the privacy of U.S. citizens. Amie Stepanovich, a legal counsel for the Electronic Privacy Information Center, said that the usc of drones by federal agencies could lead to an overall increase in the surveillance of ordinary citizens.

"They make surveillance cheaper," Stepanovich said in a phone interview. "So where it costs so many hundreds of thousands or millions of dollars to purchase and operate a helicopter, doing the same thing with a drone is significantly cheaper."

"The largest, single [civil] drone fleet that we know of is operated by Customs and Border Protection," she added. "Those licenses are very limited. It took a long time to get them. There was a lot of process involved. They also were not public, so they could be operated without much public accountability or any transparency."

A problem also arises with the amount of data that CBP's Predator program collects over time, according to Jennifer Lynch, an attorney with the Electronic Frontier Foundation.

"I think one of our biggest concerns is what any of these agencies are doing with their data after they obtain it," Lynch said in a phone interview. "Storage is so inexpensive that law enforcement and federal agencies could just maintain a library of videos of all the surveillance missions that they're doing."

"That's incredibly problematic because it means the government could go back through that library of information at any time," she explained. "What we would love to see, is if CBP and other agencies had a policy on deleting the data after a certain period of time."

At this time, CBP has not described any policy for deleting videos of Predator surveillance footage, although similar policies exist for some law enforcement agencies when collecting photographs of vehicle license plates.

Lynch also said the use of drones will mark an increase in surveillance of U.S. citizens who happen to live in areas patrolled by CBP aircraft.

"There's a huge percentage of the United States that lives on the border," Lynch said. "Congress members are proposing legislation that will protect privacy by requiring a warrant for using drones for any law enforcement investigation—but it won't require a warrant for border search purposes."

Lynch said the drone program's impact on regular citizens will be much broader than anticipated.

The use of drones for surveillance of border areas came to a head in North Dakota in June of 2011. In the first known case to involve the use of drones to arrest a U.S. citizen, Rodney Brossart, a farmer from Nelson County, N.D., was apprehended with the aid of a CBP Predator aircraft.

The situation arose after Brossart located several cattle that had wandered from a neighboring farm onto his own. He allegedly refused to return the livestock until the owner paid him for the feed and shelter he had provided during the time he held the cattle. When authorities were called in, the situation reportedly led to an armed standoff.

At one point, a nearby CBP Predator aircraft was alerted to the situation and aided in a local SWAT team's intervention. Footage from the aircraft constituted evidence in the court case, although it remained confidential, according to Brossart.

"I think it was rather ridiculous," he said in a phone interview. "You think this was the first time people in the country had their cattle get out of their fence? They wandered off, and they wandered onto another person's property. The next thing you know, there's a drone being used."

"We're in North Dakota, for Pete's sake," Brossart said. "This is very peculiar to me."

Despite concerns brought up by privacy organizations and the GAO and OIG reports, Customs and Border Protection officials still express pride in the Predator fleet.

According to Tom Salter, the director of CBP's National Air Security Operations Center in Corpus Christi, the drone program has given agents unprecedented support in halting cross-border drug shipments. He said that almost 22,000 pounds of narcotics were seized last year through the support of the drone program in Texas alone.

"We have good communication with the agents on the ground," Salter said. "They are thrilled to have us overhead while they are in the brush getting eaten up by mosquitos."

For Daniel Tirado, a Border Patrol agent on the Texas-Mexico border, these issues can be matters of life and death.

"Agents can get dehydrated and disoriented," he explained during a ride-along on the Rio Grande. "You get disoriented in the middle of the brush; how can you tell somebody where you're at and get some help?"

He said the aircraft are at the ready to help agents in danger.

Situations can also quickly arise when smugglers attempt to escape in trucks full of drugs or other contraband, leading to a vehicle pursuit by Border Patrol agents.

"Most of those don't end up pretty," Tirado said.

In recent years, smugglers have rammed Border Patrol vehicles or used caltrops—small, spiked clusters of nails that can puncture tires and potentially flip a pursuing vehicle. In such cases, unmanned aircraft can follow the escaping vehicle—for hours, if necessary—and alert agents on the ground.

Still, some industry advocates wonder if Border Patrol agents might be better served by using smaller, hand-launched drones similar to those used by the U.S. Army in overseas operations for short-range surveillance.

Ben Gielow, a government relations manager with the Association for Unmanned Vehicle Systems International, noted border surveillance is a market that manufacturers of smaller drones hope to capture.

"They've already proven their worth," Gielow said in a phone interview. "There's certainly opportunity at the smaller end of the platform."

He said "backpack-able, small, unmanned aircraft" were a quickly approaching possibility for Border Patrol agents in the field.

"Oftentimes, agents are going out and responding to a sensor or maybe a report of a sighting, and they're going out and they're not really sure what they're going to come upon," Gielow said. "Oftentimes, they won't find out until they get right up on whomever they're tracking. If you had a small unmanned aerial vehicle that they could deploy using different cameras or sensors, they could determine if those folks are armed. That kind of information could allow them to make better choices that could save lives or protect officers."

The Department of Homeland Security has recently opened a Request for Information through the Federal Business Opportunities site, specifically asking for performance specifications for small, unmanned aircraft, such as those that could be hand-launched from the backs of trucks.

The site asks drone manufacturers to "solicit participation in the Robotic Aircraft for Public Safety project from the small unmanned aerial systems (SUAS) for transition to its customers."

When asked for comment, a spokesman for the Department of Homeland Security's Science and Technology Directorate stated, "DHS does not intend to expand its use of unmanned aerial systems beyond its current mission scope."

DHS did not confirm or deny if the agency would seek small unmanned aircraft for future use.

For Border Patrol officers on the ground, any aircraft, unmanned or manned, is a critical asset, according to agent Daniel Tirado.

"Any additional resources that we get are always welcome," Tirado said. "Any equipment that we get is always good. I don't think an agent will say 'no' to any additional tool that you give them. You give them more tools, they're going to welcome it because it makes the job a lot easier. If you give them bionic vision, they'll take it."

Drones Help Track Illegal Activity on US Borders

Dan Gunderson

Dan Gunderson is based in Moorhead, Minnesota, and covers northwest Minnesota and North Dakota for MPR News.

The unmanned aircraft flying over eastern North Dakota on a cold February morning isn't the kind you'd fly in your back yard.

The Predator is about the size of a small private aircraft.

Brian Franke is one of two pilots sitting in a metal shipping container in the corner of a large noisy concrete room on the Grand Forks Air Force Base. In front of the pilots are a half dozen video screens, aircraft cockpit controls and a computer keyboard.

They're running a training mission for the U.S. Customs and Border Protection department, scanning a highway for cars. They are learning how to track moving vehicles with the aircraft's camera. Two trainers hover nearby, offering advice and correction.

"If you fly unmanned aircraft for CBP, you come here for training," said Max Raterman, Director of Air Operations in Grand Forks. The border patrol department has nine Predator drones in circulation, two of which are based out of Grand Forks. Franke will work on the United States-Mexico border when he completes his Predator flight training.

Raterman oversees 17 pilots—trained to fly helicopters, fixed-wing aircraft and the Predator drone — at Customs and Border Protection's ground control station in Grand Forks.

Pilots in Grand Forks often fly drones that are in the air over Arizona or Texas.

"Drone Patrol: Unmanned Craft Find Key Role In U.S. Border Security," Dan Gunderson, Grand Forks, N.D, Minnesota Public Radio, February 19, 2015. Reprinted by permission.

Raterman says his team's missions on the country's southern border are a priority, while flights on the northern border usually happen "when they're not busy with other stuff."

The drone is mostly used to look for signs of illegal border crossings. The Predator carries radar that can track moving people or vehicles over a wide area and tell what direction they're moving.

Raterman points to grainy gray radar pictures from a second radar that can detect footprints or tire tracks. One image shows a radar sweep of an area along the border. An image of the same area from 48 hours later shows a clearly visible white path.

"And they can see that somebody crossed on foot. That's where those red arrows are," Raterman said. "That wasn't there before. So who that is and why they did it we can't tell you that. But at least you know to watch that area."

The Predator also has a video camera, but Raterman says it can't read your license plate and it doesn't have facial recognition. And there are no weapons on the drones, although radar units look a lot like a missile hanging from the wing.

"When you demystify this stuff there's a great big collective yawn," he said. "The better story is 'they got a missile on there, or they got something that can tell your face.' There's no truth to it."

There are much higher quality cameras used, for example, on military drones, but Raterman says Customs and Border Protection doesn't use them. In addition to training and border missions, the drones based in Grand Forks sometimes help state and local officials.

They've flown missions for sheriffs in North Dakota and Minnesota, the state department of public safety and the DNR. Predator drones also monitor flood water on the Red River using radar images to look for changing conditions like ice jams.

From their desks or in the field, state and local officials can access what the drone sees using what's called a Big Pipe account. It allows a sheriff or Bureau of Criminal Apprehension agent to sign in and watch real-time video and radar images.

It's unclear how often they assist other agencies; a CBP official says there were a handful of cases in the past year.

Use of unmanned aircraft on the borders recently came under fire in a Department of Homeland Security Office of Inspector General report that concluded the drone program wasn't effective and didn't provide a good return on investment because it didn't increase arrests, and didn't fly enough missions.

"The Predator is not going to be the end-all, be-all for border security. It's a piece of a larger system," said Assistant CBP Commissioner Tex Alles.

The drone's radar, he says, can sweep a large area of the border and direct a helicopter or agents on the ground to arrest people. "No other platform I have in air marine or CBP provides me with this kind of information about a big area of what's happening on the border," Alles said. "So I think it's very advantageous."

The drone program returned $66,000 per hour of flight time during 2013, the year examined by the inspector general, Alles added. "That year the Predator system was responsible for $341 million of contraband seizures—drugs, money, weapons."

Other reports have raised privacy concerns about drone use along the border. Are they gathering data on citizens?

Alles says privacy is a concern. But he says people often confuse those larger unmanned aircraft with small drones flying close to the ground. Alles said he doesn't have the same concerns about Predator drones flying at 19,000 feet.

"The Predator system is a bigger, high-altitude system and is not probably as ubiquitous as people think it is," he says. "It's not everywhere all the time."

Alles says CBP doesn't plan to add more unmanned aircraft, but they are adding new sensors, like improved radar to the existing fleet of nine drones.

It will probably be a couple of years before the radar that can identify people and vehicles will be used on the northern border. They also plan to make improvements like de-icing equipment and improved landing gear so the Predator is better able to fly in bad weather.

Border Drones Are a Waste of Resources

Meredith Hoffman

*Meredith Hoffman is a journalist whose work has appeared in Slate,
the* New York Times, *and* Vice News. *She is immigration contributor
to* Vice.

The US may have wasted millions of dollars on drones that have ineffectively patrolled the Mexico border, a scathing Homeland Security report has revealed.

The US Customs and Border Protection's (CBP) drone surveillance program—which allegedly helped law enforcement make only 2 percent of its border arrests in 2013—follows a distressing pattern of rapid border security investment with little oversight, analysts told VICE News.

The report, released by the Department of Homeland Security's (DHS) Office of the Inspector General Tuesday, found that CBP spent at least $62.5 million on the program in one year.

DHS also found that CBP officials had vastly underreported the program's cost, claiming the unmanned aerial vehicles cost $2,468 per hour of flight time, while the inspector general calculated the real cost to be more than five times that amount, at $12,255 per hour.

"We see no evidence that the drones contribute to a more secure border, and there is no reason to invest additional taxpayer funds at this time," Inspector General John Roth said in a statement. "Securing our borders is a crucial mission for CBP and DHS. CBP's drone program has so far fallen far short of being an asset to that effort."

The inspector general's office further advised CBP to "reconsider its plan to expand" the drone program and planned additional investment of $443 million, "and put those funds to better use."

"US Drone Border Patrol Program a Huge Waste of Money, Homeland Security Report Reveals," Meredith Hoffman, *Vice News*, January 8, 2015. Reprinted by permission.

"The language of this government report is uncharacteristically blunt for a government report, and that evidences real concern from the inspector general," Mark Noferi, an enforcement fellow with the American Immigration Council, told VICE News, adding that the CBP exercised a concerning lack of discretion in operating its drone program.

The inspector general previously released a report on CPB's drone program back in 2012, which warned that the agency was "at risk of having invested significant resources in a program that… limits its ability to achieve Office of Air and Marine mission goals."

"We see this as part of a pattern," said Noferi of the latest report. "Border patrol is spending hundreds of millions and billions of dollars on increased enforcement, without evidence that increased enforcement is working the way it's intended to. There's been this explosion of border patrol funding, and often when they expand that rapidly there's inadequate oversight."

The drones further reflect the border agency's unwarranted reliance on military technology, Tony Payan, director of the Mexico Center at Rice University's Baker Institute for Public Policy, told VICE News.

"There is among border agencies, a desire to play with the latest toys developed by the military," Payan said. "They seem to have a penchant for trying to acquire hardware that doesn't really belong in the context of what they do."

Payan said that such technology, including heavy weaponry and military-style vehicles, "seems to distract [the agency] from their true mission, which is to ensure that the borders on the ground —the true threat— are fully protected and managed effectively."

CBP spokesman Carlos Lazo told VICE News Thursday that the inspector general's report was misleading and had inaccurately calculated the cost of operating the drones.

Lazo said the inspector general calculated an additional $10,000 per hour cost of the drones in his report, which included the salaries of multiple people involved in operating the technology.

But those salaries had already been included elsewhere in CBP's budget, Lazo claimed.

As for the report's claims of the ineffectiveness of the program, Lazo argued that the aircraft were used to identify "hot spots" so border patrol agents could then move to arrest people on the ground.

"It's not a silver bullet, it's one of many pieces," Lazo said of a drone's role in patrol.

In a letter sent in response to the inspector general's assessment, CBP also denied that it was planning to add another 14 aircraft, as the report claimed, and said the additional $443 million in funds would instead be used to improve and maintain its current fleet of nine drones, and to replace a lost one.

The report also "overlooked" the significant accomplishments of the program, such as its role in the seizure of $122 million worth of marijuana and $562 million worth of cocaine on the Southwest border, the letter claimed.

But analysts maintain that using drones in border policing is an expensive strategy and that the program's small gains may not outweigh its hefty price tag.

"Unmanned systems operating on the border provide an additional layer of surveillance, but once a target is identified, additional assets—including conventional reconnaissance assets — are often queued to the area to examine the target," Bill French, a policy analyst for the National Security Network, told VICE News. "That additional layer of expensive, unmanned reconnaissance may simply not be worth it."

"Drones, despite their popular appeal, aren't a cure-all, and require the right operational niche, expertise and operational environment to be effective and worth the cost," he added.

The Use of UAVs on the Border Should Be Discontinued

Arthur Holland Michel

Arthur Holland Michel is the founder of an interdisciplinary research and art group on drones at Bard College.

In 1916, the 1st Aero Squadron of the U.S. Army crossed the U.S. border into Mexico in pursuit of Pancho Villa. Their mission was to provide aerial reconnaissance for General Pershing's cavalry force. It was the first time the United States used aircraft in support of a military action. The operation was plagued with technical difficulties and adverse weather conditions; only two of the original eight aircraft returned to Texas. Today, almost one hundred years later, a fleet of unmanned aircraft operated by the U.S. Customs and Border Protection (CBP) surveil the same remote landscape over which some of America's first aviators made history. The CBP drones represent the federal government's most sustained and substantial domestic drone program.

Just as in the early days of manned aviation, the Southern borderlands have not been exactly hospitable to the prospects of unmanned flight. Since the first test flight in 2004, the CBP's drone program has been rife with operational challenges and political controversies. A recent Department of Homeland Security report on the CBP's drone operations concluded that the drone program isn't worth the time or cost. Here's what you need to know about the CBP drones:

- The Office of Border Patrol, a subset of the Department of Homeland Security's Bureau of Customs and Border Protection, started thinking about drones when it launched an ambitious remote sensing project in 1998 called the

"Customs and Border Protection Drones," Arthur Holland Michel, Center for the Study of the Drone, January 7, 2015. Reprinted by permission.

Integrated Surveillance Intelligence System—ISIS. The idea was to create a virtual border fence by erecting poles with cameras along the most high-trafficked areas of the border. Much of the thousands of miles of U.S. land borders is in remote or inaccessible areas. Remote sensing systems—that is, systems that could gather data without having a human physically present at the controls—were deemed an obvious solution to this problem.

- The ISIS program was plagued with technical difficulties and cost overruns. A 2005 report by the DHS Office of Inspector General criticized the CBP at length for failing to develop any metrics to evaluate the effectiveness of the program. In 2006, after spending $439 million, the DHS cancelled ISIS due to comprehensive system failures. In 2011, SBInet—the successor to ISIS—was also cancelled after a critical DHS review of the $1 billion program. In these reports, drones were proposed as a possible alternative to fixed sensor stations due to their endurance and mobility.

- After a year of planning, the CBP first tested a drone over the southern border between June and September 2004. The CBP used an Elbit Hermes 450, an Israeli-made, medium-sized reconnaissance and surveillance UAV. In a November 2004 report of the tests obtained by MuckRock, David V. Aguilar, then chief of the Border Patrol, concluded that while the drones were neither as operationally effective nor as cost effective as a manned helicopter, they could still be a justifiable purchase because of the future potential of unmanned aircraft. The Predator drone was estimated to be 4.6 times more expensive per flight hour than the Hermes 450 and 10 times more expensive than the Astar Helicopter. (This was not, incidentally, the first time the U.S. flew drones along its borders. According to Richard Whittle in *Predator: The Secret Origins of the Drone Revolution*, in 1995 a Predator drone was briefly used in a counter-drug exercise on the southern border.)

- The first CBP Predator took flight along the border with Mexico in October 2005. It crashed into a hillside near Nogales, Arizona in April 2006 after the contractor flying the aircraft shut down its engine mid-flight. A National Traffic and Safety Board investigation of the crash—the first ever investigation into an accident involving an unmanned aircraft—found a number of technical and operational problems with the CBP drone program.

Customs and Border Protection maintains a fleet of nine General Atomics Predator B and Guardian drones. The program is operated by the CBP's Office of Air and Marine (OAM).

- Three aircraft are based in Sierra Vista, Arizona, three are based in Grand Forks, North Dakota, and three are based in Corpus Christi, Texas. In November, 2012, the CBP proposed the acquisition of 14 additional drones at a cost of $443 million.
- The drones are used "to conduct missions in areas that are remote, too rugged for ground access, or otherwise considered too high-risk for manned aircraft or personnel on the ground."
- The CBP drones, which fly at altitudes between 19,000 ft. and 28,000 ft., are equipped with a sensor suite that includes an electro-optical and infrared camera. The sensors allow the CBP to collect footage in day or night, as well as track the movement of vehicles such as cars and boats and gather terrain information. At the minimum altitude of 19,000 ft., the CBP claims that its sensors are not powerful enough to discern a person's physical characteristics or read a license plate. The CBO also notes that its sensors cannot see through walls.
- One of the CBP drones is equipped with a Wide Area Surveillance System, which is mounted on the wing of the aircraft. This system allows the CBP to record an area approximately 3.7 miles wide.

According to a Government Accountability Office report published in September 2014, CBP drones are used for three roles:

- Patrol: drones fly on routine patrols, looking for the illegal crossing of goods or people across U.S. borders.
- Investigations: drones are used to "provide aerial support for law enforcement activities and investigations"
- Disaster response: drones are used to support emergency response to disasters such as wildfires and flooding. Drones can be used to assess the extent of damage and aid in the planning of disaster response.

While the border patrol drones fly primarily along the southern border, the CBP also stations drones in North Dakota and Florida.

- According to the Government Accountability Office report, between Fiscal Year 2011 and April 2014, 80% of drone flights occurred along border or coastal areas. The CBP clocked 18,089 hours on its drone fleet during this time: 57% of these flight hours took place over the southern border, 18% took place over the Northern border, and 7% took place over the Southeast maritime border.
- The CBP drones are not used exclusively for border patrol. According to that same GAO report, of the remaining 20%, CBP drones flew 1,726 flight hours, or 9% of the total hours, over "restricted and foreign airspace." Another 1,594 flight hours represented training, transit, and disaster response operations.
- CBP offers its drones for air support missions to other agencies within the Department of Homeland Security, such as the Drug Enforcement Agency, as well as other Federal Agencies, such as the FBI. A 2013 investigation by the Electronic Frontier Foundation found that between 2010 and 2012, CBP drones flew 500 flights for other U.S. law enforcement agencies and sheriff departments. According to a detailed Privacy Impact Assessment produced by the DHS, in such operations CBP drones could, for example, "conduct

surveillance over a building to inform ground units of the general external layout of the building or provide the location of vehicles or individuals outside the building. When flying a UAS in support of another component or government agency for an investigative operation, CBP may provide the other agency with a direct video feed through access controls or with a downloaded video recording of the operation."

- In January, 2014, CBP pilots operating one of its "Guardian" variants of the Predator drone off the coast of San Diego, California detected a malfunction and decided to ditch the unmanned aircraft in the ocean. Parts of the drone, which had been based in Arizona, were later recovered by the Coast Guard.

In a report published on May 30, 2012, the DHS Office of Inspector General concluded that the CBP drone program was poorly organized and needed to be better planned to maximize its resources. The report noted that the CBP needed to improve its coordination efforts with other agencies, especially with regards to obtaining reimbursements for costs incurred during operations in which CBP drones were used by other agencies.

On December 24, 2014, the Department of Homeland Security published a report based on an audit of the CBP's drone operations. The report concludes that the CBP drone program does not perform to expectations and is not worth the cost. The report notes that:

- The CBP drones are supposed to be airborne for 16 hours every day. In 2013, the aircraft were only airborne for about 3.5 hours per day, on average. The CBP notes that it does not fly its drones in severe weather, high winds, or when there is cloud cover.
- The CBP could only attribute "relatively few" apprehensions of illegal border crossers to its unmanned aircraft operations.
- The CBP could not demonstrate to the auditors that the use of drones has reduced the cost of border surveillance. The CBP had predicted that the use of drones would reduce the cost of border surveillance by 25% to 50% per mile.

- The CBP drones did not prove that they were able to reduce the need for Border Patrol agents to respond to incidents on the ground.
- The CBP drones focused primarily on just 170 miles of the the 1,993-mile Southwest border.
- The audit found that in 2013 the CBP drone program cost $62.5 million.

The authors write in the conclusion of the report, "Given that, after 8 years of operations, the UAS program cannot demonstrate its effectiveness, as well the cost of current operations, OAM should reconsider its planned expansion of the program. CBP could put the $443 million it plans to spend to expand the program to better use by investing in alternatives, such as manned aircraft and ground surveillance assets."

Documents and Reports

2004 Study of CBP UAV Tests in Arizona.

2005 DHS Office of Inspector General report on ISIS remote-sensing surveillance program.

2006 DHS UAS/UAV Technical Specifications.

2007 NTSB investigation of the 2006 CBP Predator drone crash.

2010 CBP Concept of Operations Report for drone operations.

2011 DHS Review of SBInet program.

2012 DHS Office of Inspector General report on CBP drone program.

2013 Investigation into the loans of CBP drones to other agencies by the Electronic Frontier Foundation.

2013 DHS Privacy Impact Assessment for the Aircraft Systems.

2014 CBP Report on the crash of a Guardian UAV.

2014 Government Accountability Office report on CBP drone program 2011-2014.

2014 DHS Office of Inspector General report on CBP drone program.

Border Drones Are Costly and Ineffective

Tom Barry

Tom Barry is a senior policy analyst at the Center for International Policy, where he directs the TransBorder Project. Barry specializes in immigration policy, homeland security, border security, and the outsourcing of national security.

President Obama and Homeland Security Secretary Jeh Johnson are committed to more drone surveillance of US borders. Over the past year, the president has called for emergency supplemental funding for DHS to fund a "sustained border security surge," including new funding for border drones.

Johnson specified that deployment of Predator drones over the Southwest border is key to his new "border security initiative, which he calls the Southern Border and Approaches Campaign. Before joining DHS last year, Johnson served successively as general counsel for the Air Force and Department of Defense (2009-2013). As the chief DOD legal counsel, Johnson formulated the legal justification for President Obama's use of Predator drones in targeted killings overseas.

Support by the White House and DHS for the use of military-grade drones persists even as criticism of the program mounts. Since the first deployment in 2005 of Predator drones by Customs and Border Protection (CBP)—the most generously funded DHS agency—the program has come under critical review from the Congressional Research Service, Government Accountability Office (GAO), and the DHS Office of the Inspector General (OIG).

More than a dozen reports have lambasted the drone program for its failure to meet stated goals, absence of performance measures, and failure to formulate operational plans and strategic

"Dysfunctional Drones Underscore Mission Mess at Homeland Security," Tom Barry, Truthout, January 21, 2015. Reprinted by permission.

directions. Office of Air and Marine (OAM), which DHS created at the same time that CBP launched the drone program, has overseen the expansion of its drone fleet from one Predator to eight Predators and two Predator marine-surveillance variants known as Guardians.

As part of its strategic plan, CBP/OAM plans to increase the drone fleet to two-dozen Predators and Guardians—a plan that allows CBP/OAM to respond to emergencies and threats anywhere within the United States in three hours or less.

CBP has been largely dismissive of governmental evaluations of its border drone program. In 2012, the DHS inspector general produced a report that added to the growing library of critical evaluations of the border drones, taking CBP/OAM to task for its lack of performance measures and for keeping the Predators grounded on military bases rather than flying surveillance missions.

This scathing evaluation didn't undermine White House or DHS support for the costly drone program. And CBP/OAM essentially shrugged off the OIG's critiques and recommendations —as is evident in a new OIG evaluation

The recently released report (published in December 2014 and made public in early January 2015) is the harshest of governmental evaluations of the troubled drone program to date. "Notwithstanding the significant investment, we see no evidence that the drones contribute to a more secure border, and there is no reason to invest additional taxpayer funds at this time," the report concludes.

The OIG report hammers the CBP and the Office of Air and Marine for the continuing failure to institute performance measures and to meet planned flight-time objectives. What is more, OIG takes CBP/OAM to task for its deception regarding the costs of the drone program and the area of the border subject to drone surveillance. Furthermore, the report notes the program's meager results and its failure to reduce the overall costs of border control, as CBP has repeatedly promised.

The report also takes CBP/OAM to task for not providing a full accounting of the costs of the drone program and observes that the program has fallen far short of its stated goals in terms of flight time, apprehensions, reducing costs of border control, and area covered by drone surveillance.

The report falls short of calling for DHS to shut down the CBP drone program, but did take the unusual step of calling for an independent investigation of it.

CBP resistance to oversight and reform has been increasingly on display as it has been subject to a steady stream of critical media reports and government investigations, notably with respect to its human rights abuses and shoddy investigations of Border Patrol killings of immigrants.

The report highlights the enormous waste of government funds spent on border drones while underscoring the program's complete absence of strategic direction. But still more shocking is the OIG report's revelations about CBP's near-total lack of accountability and transparency—and honesty.

Drones for Border Counterterrorism

In the wake of the September 11, 2001, terrorist attacks, President George W. Bush authorized CBP to launch a drone surveillance program using Predator drones manufactured by General Atomics. Initial steps to kick off the drone surveillance program occurred in 2004 when General Atomics gave CBP a demonstration of a Predator drone in Arizona.

Before entering into its purchasing, operation and maintenance contracts with General Atomics, CBP didn't study how drones could contribute to border control or review the type of drones that could best meet the gaps in border surveillance. Instead, CBP looked to the national security establishment for guidance and determined that the same drones favored by the military and the CIA for surveillance and targeted killings in the Middle East and South Asia could help secure the US border.

The first unarmed Predator began patrolling the border the next year. It was also in 2005 that DHS created OAM to manage CBP's aerial and marine assets.

To direct the newly created Office of Air and Marine, DHS appointed Michael C. Kostelnik, a retired Air Force major general, who oversaw its drone procurement from General Atomics. Kostelnik resigned in late 2012, and was succeeded by retired Maj. Gen. Randolph Alles. Other retired military officers have also dominated the leadership ranks of OAM since the agency's founding and since the creation of the drone program.

Counterterrorism has been the explicit mission and No. 1 stated priority of CBP's drone program, which, according to CBP, "focuses operations on the CBP priority mission of anti-terrorism by helping to identify and intercept potential terrorists and illegal cross-border activity."

This counterterrorism mission and military ties might help explain why DHS has permitted CBP to rely on one supplier for its drones and has not subjected drone purchasing to open bidding. Since 2004, CBP has maintained sole-source contracts with General Atomics for the Predator and Guardian drones.

Expensive and Ineffective

With barely contained contempt, the OIG's report focuses on three specific problem areas: 1) lack of performance measures and lack of results, 2) the disguised costs of running a program and the alarming absence of any cost-benefit evaluations, and 3) the deception and duplicity of CBP, the operations of which are only a faint shadow of what CBP says its drones do.

Two documents—Concept of Operations (CONOPS) and UAS (Unmanned Aerial Systems) Mission Statement—do provide a framework for OAM operations, including the drone program. CONOPS, however, is more a description of operational goals —such as "operating over land borders and over coastal waters" and "working with the Federal Aviation Administration" to open more national airspace to DHS drones—than a plan that links operations to strategic goals.

The OIG found no evidence that CBP/OAM has formulated performance measures that would allow DHS to determine that the drone program has indeed contributed to any increase in border security. "CBP has invested significant funds in a program that has not achieved the expected results, and it cannot demonstrate how much the program has improved border security," the OIG concluded.

Much to the consternation of the GAO and OIG, CBP has tacitly declined—without explicitly refusing—to compare the effectiveness of the various instruments of its border control mission.

In the case of OAM, for example, it has never compared the varying effectiveness and cost-benefit ratios of its more than two-dozen types of aircraft - from light turbo-prop planes and one-pilot helicopters, to the P-3 all-weather surveillance planes, Black Hawk helicopters, and Predator and Guardian drones. Nor has CBP/OAM evaluated the comparative effectiveness of drones, ranging from ones that can be hauled in the back of Border Patrol pickups to the multimillion-dollar drones it purchases from the major military contractor General Atomics.

In the past, CBP regularly released apprehension and drug seizure statistics purporting to demonstrate the effectiveness of the drone program. But the low number of immigrant apprehensions, the failure of CBP to prove that these immigrants were "transnational criminals" as it claimed and the paltry quantity of illegal drugs (exclusively marijuana) undermined rather than supported CBP's case for drones. What is more, CBP would not clarify whether these arrests and seizures would have occurred without drone involvement and CBP declined to provide any way to verify its numbers of purported apprehensions and arrests.

CBP did provide the OIG with apprehension and drug seizure numbers "associated" with the drone program. But the small numbers did nothing to bolster CBP's argument that drones are essential for effective border control. According to OIG, the extent of increased apprehensions of undocumented border crossers is uncertain, but compared to CBP's total number of apprehensions, OAM attributed relatively few to unmanned aircraft operations. Furthermore, the report noted that interviews with Border Patrol agents suggest that most of the cited apprehensions would have occurred without drone surveillance.

Although the CBP/OAM drone program has been operating since 2005, the total costs of the program remain unknown because of CBP's continuing failure to release a full accounting of the funds allocated to purchase, maintain and operate the drones. Also missing in the accounting are the costs of reviewing the thousands of hours of surveillance footage.

Sloppy accounting and CBP/OAM secrecy have made it impossible to determine the full cost of the program.

CBP has consistently lowballed the costs of operating drones, stating that it costs about $2,500 per hour while actual cost is $12,250. CBP didn't include such key costs as operator salaries, overhead and the payloads (surveillance and communications devices) the drones carry. The OIG found that CIP/OAM spent $62.5 million in 2013 to operate its drones—about five times as much as the CBP reported.

Since 2004, CBP has purchased 11 Predator drones (including two Guardians). It has lost two of these $18-20 million drones in crashes, and currently operates nine drones along the northern and southern borders, and over the Atlantic and Pacific approaches to the United States.

The OIG found that OAM put drones in the air only 22 percent of the time it had projected. CBP pointed to two problems that limit flight time: bad weather (drones cannot be flown in bad weather or when there is cloud cover) and shortages in piloting and maintenance crews. But keeping drones grounded most of the time might also be attributed to CBP/OAM's inability to find a constructive use for the drone fleet.

CBP routinely declares that the drones operated by OAM conduct surveillance over the entire Southwest border. However,

OIG found that virtually all of the flights in 2013 were limited to a 100-mile section of the Arizona border and a 70-mile segment of the Texas border.

As part of its conclusions, OIG stated: "Given the cost of the Unmanned Aircraft System program and its unproven effectiveness, CBP should reconsider its plan to expand the program. The $443 million that CBP plans to spend [by way of sole-source contracts with General Atomics] on program expansion could be put to better use by investing in alternatives, such as manned aircraft and ground surveillance assets," OIG observed.

Changing Objectives of Drone Surveillance

Since the start of the drone program, CBP and OAM have struggled to describe how exactly drone surveillance contributes to improved border control.

Promising constant surveillance of the border by drones, CBP/OAM officials have repeatedly asserted in congressional testimony that drones are "force-multipliers"—meaning that they would improve the performance of the Border Patrol agents by relaying images of undocumented border crossers to agents in the field.

But CBP/OAM was never able to document this force-multiplier effect, and OIG found no evidence drones resulted in lower costs or improvement in Border Patrol efficiency. According to the UAS (Unmanned Aerial Systems) Mission Need Statement, OAM expected unmanned aircraft to reduce border surveillance costs by 25 to 50 percent per mile. But OAM does not track this metric or any other, OIG observed, and consequently cannot demonstrate that the unmanned aircraft have reduced the cost of border surveillance.

Another common description of drone operations offered by CBP/OAM was that drones did not fly aimlessly over the border, but mostly responded to alerts from ground sensors. But CBP/OAM was unable to document the success of this drone operation strategy, and later acknowledged that ground sensors were unreliable indicators of illegal border crossings.

Over the past couple of years, CBP/OAM has offered a new description of drone operations. Rather than spotting undocumented border crossers or responding to ground sensors, drone surveillance provides "change detection capability." Repeated flights by drones over the same areas of the border allow the Border Patrol to identify "emergent threats" by detecting changes along the border, such as cut fences or tire tracks.

However, the surveillance systems on the unmanned aerial systems purchased from General Atomics do not provide the detailed images that would permit successful "change detection." CBP/OAM's solution has been to increase its drone program spending by buying a radar sensor system called Vehicle and Dismount Exploitation Radar (VADER).

The system was developed for use in Iraq and Afghanistan to give the military and CIA the ability to distinguish humans from animals in high altitudes and to direct cameras to track the targeted humans and vehicles. CBP began including VADER in its drone program in 2011 when the Department of Defense loaned the agency two systems.

According to Northrup Grumman, the manufacturer of the VADER systems, VADER allows "accurate Ground Moving Target Indicator (GMTI) and Synthetic Aperture Radar (SAR) imagery to be readily available to ground commanders in real time."

One problem with the VADER system is its cost. CBP/OAM bought two VADERs for $16.8 million. In addition, CBP spent $1.7 million in contract support for one year. According to OIG, CBP/OAM plans to buy four more VADER sensors along with the necessary contracted operational support.

Boasting of its new surveillance capacity, CBP stated in 2012 that VADER systems would "dramatically" affect border operations in Arizona, New Mexico and Texas.

Sen. John McCain (R-Arizona) hailed CBP's acquisition of the VADER systems, calling them "an incredible technology tool." But problems other than their high cost undercut CBP's argument that VADER systems will boost border security. Contrary to what CBP promised, the radar sensors have been limited to a small stretch of the border patrolled by one Border Patrol station.

What is more, CBP is at a loss to describe their worth. Summing up the effectiveness problem of the VADERs, OIG observed that "CBP's Office of Intelligence and Investigative Liaison (OIIL) could not analyze the sensor data as described in CBP's June 2012 VADER CONOPS to determine entry points, trails, and fence breakthroughs along other areas of the border."

Immigration and Drones Closely Linked

CBP and OAM assert that drone missions are "risk-based." However, despite the continued rhetorical commitment to counterterrorism as its primary mission, CBP rarely refers to terrorism when describing border operations. Instead, when CBP refers to risks, it points to the sections of the border with the most undocumented immigration.

As the OIG report makes clear, the CBP drone program is immigrant-focused. There is not one mention in the recent report of the drone program's role in counterterrorism. The only concrete result of the drone program cited by CBP and the OIG was the small number of immigrants purportedly apprehended with the assistance of drone surveillance. OIG, however, noted that Border Patrol agents interviewed by investigators observed that these immigrants likely would have been apprehended without drone assistance.

The expansion of the border drone program, however, has been less tied to the apprehension of immigrants in the US borderlands than to US immigration policy.

Since 2001, the Bush and Obama administrations have launched an array of new initiatives to demonstrate their commitment to "securing the border." Generally, these initiatives have come at times of increased national anxiety about undocumented immigration, drug trafficking and drug-related violence in Mexico. Like the most prominent of these post-9/11 border security initiatives—

the Secure Border Initiative of 2005—the latest initiative is closely associated with immigration policy and its reform.

Over the past year, the Obama administration has on two occasions called for greater border security, including drone operations on the US-Mexico border: the humanitarian crisis of Central American refugees crossing the border illegally last summer, and the lead-up to and announcement of the president's executive order legalizing the immigration status of 5 million immigrants.

In the midst of the humanitarian and political crisis caused by the influx of Central American child refugees last summer, President Obama petitioned Congress for $3.7 billion in emergency funding to support a "sustained border security surge." The proposal included $39 million for increased aerial surveillance, including funding for 16 additional drone crews.

Despite an expanding library of critical evaluation reports on the high costs and dubious achievements of border drones, President Obama has repeatedly backed the border drone program in the administration's requests for increased Department of Homeland Security funding.

The president's November 2014 executive order on immigration was carefully orchestrated to include a commitment to more border security, including increased drone surveillance. In the November 20 announcement of the immigration reform order, the White House, borrowing Nixon-era rhetoric about tough law enforcement, stressed that the Obama administration would be "cracking down on illegal immigration at the border." And borrowing military language, the White House stated that the new border security surge would include a newly centralized "command-and-control" approach to securing the border.

In anticipation of the president's November 2014 executive order on immigration, DHS Secretary Jeh Johnson in October 2014 unveiled the administration's new border security plan, titled the Southern Border and Approaches Campaign.

Droning on About Border Security

The clumsily named Southern Border and Approaches Campaign offers nothing new other than more border security bureaucracy and an infusion of the latest military jargon—although promising "an even more secure border and a smart strategy to get there."

From the start of his tenure as DHS chief, Johnson has not only supported the drone program, but has also used military concepts and terminology to define the department's border security operations. Although lacking experience in border control, Johnson had been a key player in the Obama administration's use of Predator drones for targeting killings.

The border security campaign, packaged by DHS as "Border Security for the 21st Century," makes no substantive changes in border security tactics or strategy. All programs, including the failed drone program, remain part of the Southern Border and Approaches Campaign. However, if the president were to succeed in getting his supplemental funding request approved by Congress, the campaign would have at least a couple of billion dollars more to beef up existing programs.

Before his DHS appointment, Johnson served successively as general counsel for the Air Force and Defense Department. During his 2009 to 2013 tenure as chief defense department lawyer, Johnson was a firm supporter of the Obama administration's increased use of targeted drone strikes and helped develop a legal rationale for those killings, including for drone strikes targeting US citizens.

As part of the campaign, Johnson said DHS would form three new joint task forces: Joint Task Force East, Joint Task Force West and Joint Task Force Investigations. "We are discarding stove pipes," declared Johnson, explaining that the new task forces would bring together the three DHS agencies involved in immigration enforcement, customs and border protection with the Coast Guard.

Not mentioned was the fact that numerous former and existing DHS task forces have brought together all these agencies as well as others such as the FBI and DEA. The creation of these joint task forces mirrors the surge within the US armed forces in the emphasis on joint task forces and joint operations. The Doctrine for the Armed Forces of the United States (2013) uses the word "joint" 939 times.

Also contributing to the nebulous character of the Southern Border and Approaches Campaign is the use of other military terminology, such as "supported-supporting." Describing how the new task forces will function, Johnson said: "These Task Forces should adopt a supported-supporting component model." This military jargon, while not new, is gaining new currency, as is apparent in the 2013 doctrine.

Border Security on Autopilot

There are no signs as of yet that CBP, DHS, Congress or the White House is backing away from the dysfunctional and massively expensive drone program.

The border drone program has received favored treatment by Congress (both Democrats and Republicans) and the White House (both Bush and Obama), even as CBP has proved unable to demonstrate that drones are effective instruments of border control.

Widespread support in federal government for the drone program does not necessarily demonstrate a conviction that Predators on the border are fundamental to border control. Rather, it is likely an indication of the prevalence of a political dogma that holds that the more money spent on border security, the better and safer the homeland will be. For some, a corollary of this border security principle is that a continuing border security buildup makes it politically easier to pitch immigration reform.

Given the continued support—and calls for increased funding —by both parties and the executive and legislative branches, CBP's failure to revise or shut down the drone program is not surprising.

As its budget has tripled and the number of Border Patrol agents doubled, CBP has adamantly insisted that all its border control instruments—boots on the ground, 18-foot steel walls, radiation detectors, electronic fences, drones etc. are all fundamental to securing the nation's borders.

Setting realistic performance goals that can be used to measure the effectiveness of the CBP programs, as the OIG recommends, will be a major challenge for CBP and OAM—in part because it has no history of establishing performance measures.

More problematic is CBP/OAM's lack of a clear and pragmatic definition of what constitutes a secure border.

Not addressed by the report are more fundamental problems that infect DHS and its two subsidiary agencies, CBP and OAM. At least part of the problem at CBP/OAM is the absence of a clear and pragmatic mission. Symptomatic of this problem is the inability of DHS and CBP to define exactly what they mean by the terms "homeland security" and "border security," as a January 2013 report by the Congressional Research Service pointed out.

Border control since 9/11 has been framed in terms of national security and counterterrorism. This strategic shift has resulted in an overreliance on military tactics, strategies, personnel and hardware—as well as military infrastructure, such as the military bases that host the border drones. Yet the actual focus of border control is still apprehending unauthorized immigrants and seizing illegal drugs, resulting in a mismatch between the stated strategic mission and field (and air) operations.

Should Drones Be Used for Domestic Surveillance?

Overview: Responses to the Domestic Drone Surveillance Program

ACLU of Massachusetts

The ACLU of Massachusetts defends the principles enshrined in the Massachusetts Declaration of Rights as well as the US Constitution.

"[O]ur country has taken singular pride in the democratic ideals enshrined in its Constitution… It would indeed be ironic if, in the name of national defense, we would sanction the subversion of one of those liberties…which makes the defense of the Nation worthwhile."

– Chief Justice Earl Warren[1]

"[O]ur Forefather Benjamin Franklin warned against such a temptation by opining that those 'who can give up essential liberty to obtain a little temporary safety, deserve neither liberty nor safety.'"[2]

– Majority Opinion, *Tobey v. Jones*

"Preserving our freedom is one of the main reasons that we are now engaged in this new war on terrorism. We will lose that war without firing a shot if we sacrifice the liberties of the American people."

– U.S. Senator Russ Feingold, soon after the September 11, 2001 terrorist attacks[3]

Overview

Unmanned aerial vehicles, commonly known as drones, are an emerging and rapidly-expanding development in domestic surveillance technology.[4] On Valentine's Day 2012, President Barack Obama signed the FAA Modernization and Reform Act of

"Domestic Drone Surveillance Usage: Threats And Opportunities For Regulation," ACLU of Massachusetts. Reprinted by permission.

2012, legislation authorizing the Federal Aviation Administration (FAA) to develop regulations to facilitate the growing usage of drones in domestic airspace.[5]

Drones are best known for their use in military operations[6] including the use of weaponized drones for targeted killing. But drones have been used for domestic surveillance purposes for years[7] and their usage is expected to grow exponentially.[8]

The FAA has issued 1,428 drone operator permits since 2007 (as of mid-February) and predicts there will be 10,000 drones deployed within the next five years.[9] A public information request by the Electronic Frontier Foundation showed that numerous universities and law enforcement agencies have been approved to use drones by the FAA.[10]

Of course, the widespread use of drones for domestic surveillance raises serious privacy concerns.[11]

Drones can be outfitted with high definition[12] and infrared cameras,[13] and even license plate readers.[14] Drones "present unique threats to privacy," in the words of one privacy advocate.[15] Why? They are smaller—potentially insect-sized,[16] can fly longer— perhaps soon in perpetuity,[17] and are not bound by the historical, practical check on law enforcement excesses we've had as a result of limited police resources.[18]

In a seminal 1890 law review article aptly-titled The Right to Privacy, future Supreme Court Justice Louis Brandeis recognized that "instantaneous photographs…have invaded the secret precincts of private and domestic life…Of the desirability—indeed of the necessity—of some such protection there can, it is believed, be no doubt."[19] Brandeis and his co-author Samuel Warren were ahead of their time when they wrote that article but even they couldn't foresee anything like the domestic surveillance schemes that have arisen over a century later.

Drone Use in Massachusetts and Response to Boston Marathon Bombings

Late in 2012, the Boston Globe reported that a SWAT team in Massachusetts had filed an application with the FAA for a drone.[20] As of April 2013, there were no police drones yet in Massachusetts but Waltham-based defense contractor Raytheon was flying many of them in testing capacities.[21] Surveillance and war contracting companies hope to expand their market from military to domestic law enforcement.[22]

Following the explosion of two bombs at the 2013 Boston Marathon, parts of the city shut down as the search for a suspect continued, prompting Ron Paul to write: "This unprecedented move should frighten us as much or more than the attack itself."[23] Boston Police Commissioner Ed Davis told the public shortly afterward that he seeks more surveillance cameras (there are already hundreds) in downtown Boston.[24] And further, he said, he wants to have drone surveillance for next year's marathon.[25]

Responses to Drone Programs

While the acceleration of local law enforcement to military-style operations may be inevitable,[26] legislative and public opposition to drone proliferation can be successful. Already, efforts to restrict drone surveillance powers have been successful in multiple state legislatures. And communities have rebelled against the technology.

Earlier this year in Seattle, public pressure caused the Seattle Police Department to cancel its drone program.[27] Around the same time, Charlottesville, Virginia passed a law banning any use of drones by its municipal agencies, becoming the first city in the country to pass anti-drone legislation.[28]

More recently, the governor of Florida signed a drone-regulation bill, endorsed by both Republicans and the ACLU, which requires a judge to approve most drone surveillance operations (with an imminent danger exception).[29] A bill pending in Massachusetts provides similar protections.[30]

The federal government also has opportunities to act on drone privacy.

In Congress, several bills have been introduced to reign in domestic drone usage. The Preserving Freedom from Unwarranted Surveillance Act of 2013 requires a probable-cause warrant for drone surveillance, with some exceptions.[31] (Senator Rand Paul filed similar legislation during the previous session but has not re-introduced it.)

Another bill, the Preserving American Privacy Act of 2013, prohibits domestic drones except with warrants, or for border searches or emergencies. The bill also requires government entities to file detailed data collection statements about their drone surveillance.[32]

Then there's the Drone Aircraft Privacy and Transparency Act of 2013, which would amend the FAA Modernization and Reform Act of 2012, requiring a study of privacy concerns, a data collection statement for each drone operation, including a data minimization statement, and enforcement mechanisms including license revocation for violators of these requirements.[33] But some close observers, including Peter Singer of the Brookings Institution, criticize proposals that would involve the FAA in drone regulation because they argue that its priority is safety, not privacy.[34] Justice Sandra Day O'Connor had recognized this problem in a concurring opinion on aerial surveillance back in 1989.[35]

All of the above bills originate in the House, but the Senate hasn't remained silent on the issue. The Senate Judiciary Committee held a hearing in March to address the rise of domestic drones.[36]

Amidst all the discussion of how to limit government-operated drone use, there has been little conversation about the tricky prospect of regulating drones for personal civilian use. The FAA does very little to regulate private, non-commercial drone use,[37] a business which could grow quickly, and a hobby which could be co-opted by the government to skirt drone privacy rules directed at police and intelligence agencies.

Cost-Benefit Analysis

The biometrics industry is expected to be worth $10 billion within the next five years.[38] Biometric identification systems are already widely used by law enforcement[39] and are augmenting drone surveillance capabilities.[40] But not only is biometrics technology invasive, it is also notoriously unreliable.[41]

A 2010 report released by the National Research Council noted the high risk of false positives and concluded that all biometric recognition technologies are "inherently fallible."[42] A professor receiving federal government funding for biometric research, including motion pattern recognition, conceded "we should be worried" of this "Big Brother" but asserted "[w]e just have to get used to it, that we're less private citizens."[43]

Beyond its technological flaws, surveillance technology is exorbitantly expensive given its remarkable ineffectiveness. A bipartisan Senate committee report concluded the fusion centers around the country, implemented to conglomerate federal and local law enforcement resources to fight terrorism,[44] do not provide useful intelligence.[45] In the words of Senator Tom Coburn, "Instead of strengthening our counterterrorism efforts, they have too often wasted money and stepped on Americans' civil liberties."[46]

Even without the presence of drones, the sprawling dimensions of the surveillance state are vastly unprecedented. Research by John Mueller and Mark G. Stewart noted in 2012 that homeland security expenditures have exceeded $1 trillion since the September 11 attacks.[47]

John Rizzo, the man who approved much of the government's operations to fight the so called War on Terror as the top lawyer at the Central Intelligence Agency (CIA) in the first nine years after the September 11th attacks, and who spent thirty-four years in the CIA total, said: the "cumulative number" of covert operations during the cold war "pales in comparison to the number of programs, number of activities the CIA was asked to carry out in the aftermath of 9/11 in the counterterrorism area."[48]

According to a 2010 report by the Washington Post, every day the National Security Agency intercepts 1.7 billion emails and other communications.[49]

But despite all the costly data surveillance and sharing, events like the Boston Marathon bombing are still likely to occur.[50] Following the 2010 attempted Times Square bombing, one security expert wrote: "Cameras won't help. They don't prevent terrorist attacks, and their forensic value after the fact is minimal."[51]

In contrast to vast sums of money being spent on prevention, the actual likelihood of a terrorist attack is exceedingly small.[52] Followers of American counterterrorism policy have observed that the United States has overreacted.[53]

Constant drone surveillance could be the next symptom of this panic.

Finally, Orwellian measures have the potential to exacerbate the security problem by provoking resentment against the government.[54] Drone use overseas has been demonstrated to produce dangerous blowback that threatens the national security of the country, with effects that could last for decades.[55] There is evidence that the worst-case scenario is already happening: in the process of trying to fight terrorism, the government can exacerbate the terrorism problem by creating new enemies.

Conclusion

History shows that our response to threats to our physical safety mustn't involve programs or policies that diminish our core rights. Two centuries ago, during a time of great national insecurity, the War of 1812, the Constitution's primary author, President James Madison, took virtually no steps to diminish civil liberties. Madison's approach did not lead to the nation's demise.[56]

With the rise of domestic drones as a cherry on top of an already sprawling surveillance state, America is headed in the opposite direction. But there is time yet to ensure the technology doesn't trample all over our rights.

If mass drone surveillance is inescapable, warrant and data collection reporting requirements will provide a critical check against government abuses. Justice Brandeis has written, "Publicity is justly commended as a remedy for social and industrial diseases. Sunlight is said to be the best of disinfectants; electric light the most efficient policeman."[57]

Domestic drones can monitor individuals almost constantly; it's therefore essential to have sunlight shine upon their operators, to monitor their actions. The publicity necessary to hold their operations accountable to the public requires transparency and accountability.[58]

Drone usage will continue to expand and may not stop even at infrared camera surveillance and biometric data acquisition. The Guardian's Glenn Greenwald has cautioned that although domestic drones may currently be limited to those outfitted only with surveillance equipment, given the increasing militarization of domestic law enforcement, the time may come soon when domestic drones are weaponized.[59]

But even short of that futuristic nightmare, drone surveillance already poses a new threat to liberty at home. As our Fourth Amendment search protection diminishes with the progress of technology,[60] legislative initiatives and public outcry may be the only way to protect the right to privacy in the age of domestic drones.

References

1. United States v. Robel, 389 U.S. 258, 264 (1967).
2. Tobey v. Jones, 706 F.3d 379, 393 (4th Cir. 2013).
3. Speech to the U.S. Senate, Oct. 25, 2001 (quoted in Bill Moyers' Journal, PBS, Dec. 5, 2008, http://www.pbs.org/moyers/journal/12052008/transcript4.html).
4. See generally, Richard M. Thompson II, Domestic Drone Surveillence Operations: Fourth Amendment Implications and Legislative Responses, Cong. Research Serv. (Apr. 3, 2013), available at http://www.fas.org/sgp/crs/natsec/R42701.pdf; Norman Reimer, The Droning of America: Here, There and Everywhere, 37-Feb Champion 9 (Jan./Feb. 2013); Benjamin Kapnik, Unmanned but Accelerating: Navigating the Regulatory and Privacy Challenges of Introducing Unmanned Aircraft into the National Airspace System, 77 J. Air L. & Com. 439, 442-49 (2012).
5. FAA Modernization and Reform Act of 2012, Pub. L. No. 112-95, §332, 126 Stat. 11, 74; see FAA, Fact Sheet – Unmanned Aircraft Systems (UAS), Feb. 9, 2013, http://www.faa.gov/news/fact_sheets/news_story.cfm?newsId=14153. Unmanned

aircraft system encompasses the aerial vehicle as well as the digital network and human operator(s).

6. See Steve Coll, Our Drone Delusion, New Yorker, May 6, 2013, http://www.newyorker.com/arts/critics/books/2013/05/06/130506crbo_books_coll?currentPage=all; Spencer Ackerman, Welcome to the Era of Big Drone Data, Wired, Danger Room (Apr. 25, 2013), http://www.wired.com/dangerroom/2013/04/drone-sensors-big-data/; Sen. Judiciary Comm. hearing, Drone Wars: The Constitutional and Counterterrorism Implications of Targeted Killing, Apr. 23, 2013, http://www.judiciary.senate.gov/hearings/hearing.cfm?id=b01a319ecae60e7cbb832de271030205; Josh Meyer, CIA Expands Use of Drones in Terror War, L.A. Times, Jan. 29, 2006, http://articles.latimes.com/2006/jan/29/world/fg-predator29; Jack M. Beard, Law and War in the Virtual Era, 103 Am. J. Int'l L. 409 (2009) (drone use in global War on Terror goes back over a decade).

7. See, Peter Finn, Domestic use of aerial drones by law enforcement likely to prompt privacy debate, Wash. Post. Jan. 23, 2011, http://www.washingtonpost.com/wp-dyn/content/article/2011/01/22/AR2011012204111.html?wpisrc=nl_headline; Larry Copeland, Police turn to drones for domestic surveillance, USA Today, Jan. 14, 2011, http://usatoday30.usatoday.com/tech/news/surveillance/2011-01-13-drones_N.htm, Ed Lavandera, Drones silently patrol U.S. borders, CNN (Mar. 12, 2010, 7:30 PM EST), http://www.cnn.com/2010/US/03/12/border.drones/index.html?_s=PM:US; see generally,Paul McBride,Beyond Orwell: The Application of Unmanned Aircraft Systems in Domestic Surveillance Operations, 74 J. Air L. & Com. 627, 628-634 (2009).

8. See Ben Stone, ACLU of Iowa, Preparing for the Attack of the Domestic Drones, Mar. 18, 2013 http://www.aclu-ia.org/2013/03/18/preparing-for-the-attack-of-the-domestic-drones/; Editorial, The Dawning of Domestic Drones, N.Y. Times, Dec. 25, 2012,http://www.nytimes.com/2012/12/26/opinion/the-dawning-of-domestic-drones.html?_r=0.

9. SeeBrian Bennett & Joel Rubin, Drones are taking to the skies in the U.S., L.A. Times, Feb. 15, 2013 http://articles.latimes.com/2013/feb/15/nation/la-na-domestic-drones-20130216.

10. See Jennifer Lynch, FAA Releases Lists of Drone Certificates—Many Questions Left Unanswered, EFF, Apr. 19, 2012, https://www.eff.org/deeplinks/2012/04/faa-releases-its-list-drone-certificates-leaves-many-questions-unanswered; see Andy Pasztor & John Emschwiller, Drone Use Takes Off on the Home Front, Wall St. J., Apr. 21, 2012, http://online.wsj.com/article/SB10001424052702304331204577354331959335276.html.

11. See, e.g., Carrie Kahn, It's A Bird! It's A Plane! It's A Drone!, Nat'l Pub. Radio(Mar. 14, 2011 3:55 PM), http://www.npr.org/2011/03/14/134533552/its-a-bird-its-a-plane-its-a-drone, The drone over your backyard: A guide, The Week, June 8, 2012, http://theweek.com/article/index/228830/the-drone-over-your-backyard-a-guide; Robert Stanton, Texas civil libertarians have eye on police drones, Hous. Chron., Oct. 31, 2011, http://www.chron.com/news/houston-texas/article/Texas-civil-libertarians-have-eye-on-police-drones-2245644.php

12. See US Army unveils 1.8 gigapixel camera helicopter drone, BBC, (December 29, 2011 6:11p.m.), http://www.bbc.com/news/technology-16358851.

13. See Draganflyer X6, Thermal Infrared Camera, http://www.draganfly.com/uav-helicopter/draganflyer-x6/features/flir-camera.php

14. See 9 ACLU Seeks Details on Automatic License Plate Readers in Massive Nationwide Request, ACLU (July 31, 2012), http://www.aclu.org/technology-and-liberty/aclu-seeks-details-automatic-licenseplate-readers-massive-nationwide-reque-4; Customs and Border Protection Today,Unmanned Aerial Vehicles Support Border Security (July/Aug. 2004), http://www.cbp.gov/xp/CustomsToday/2004/Aug/other/aerial_vehicles.xml.

15. Using Unmanned Aircraft Systems Within the Homeland: Security Game Changers? Hearing Before Subcomm. On Oversight, Investigations, and Management of H. Comm. on Homeland Sec., 112th Cong. 3 (2012) (statement of Amie Stepanovich, Counsel. Electronic Privacy Information Center (EPIC)).

16. Mosquito-like drone at Harvard could be used to pollinate, spy on you in the shower, Privacy Matters blog (May 2, 2013, 16:17), http://www.privacysos.org/node/1047.

17. See Mark Brown, Lockheed uses ground-based laser to recharge drone mid-flight, Wired, July 12, 2012, http://www.wired.co.uk/news/archive/2012-07/12/lockheed-lasers.

18. See Thompson, supra note 4, at 16.

19. 4 Samuel D. Warren & Louis D. Brandeis, The Right to Privacy, 4 Harv. L. Rev. 193, 195, 196 (1890).

20. Scott Kirsner,Drones may soon buzz through local skies,Bos. Globe, Oct. 21, 2012, http://www.bostonglobe.com/business/2012/10/20/drone-aircraft-adapted-from-military-uses-coming-skies-near-you/h1rQ29NYRYwh0o6AIeOqDN/story.html.

21. No police drones in MA yet, but Raytheon is flying a bunch of them, Privacy Matters blog (Apr. 22, 2013, 11:47), http://www.privacysos.org/node/590.

22. See Drones: Eyes in the Sky, CBS News (Feb. 10, 2013, 9:20 AM), http://www.cbsnews.com/8301-3445_162-57568571/drones-eyes-in-the-sky/ ("Now, drones are headed off the battlefield. They're already coming your way. AeroVironment, the California company that sells the military something like 85 percent of its fleet, is marketing them now to public safety agencies.").

23. Sabrina Siddiqui, Ron Paul Shutdown After Boston Bombings More Frightening Than Attack Itself, Huffington Post (Apr. 29, 2013, 2:35 PM EDT), http://www.huffingtonpost.com/2013/04/29/ron-paul-boston-bombings_n_3179489.html?ncid=edlinkusaolp00000009.

24. Terry Atlas & Greg Stohr, Surveillance Cameras Sought by Cities After Boston Bombs, Bloomberg, Apr. 29, 2013, http://www.bloomberg.com/news/2013-04-29/surveillance-cameras-sought-by-cities-after-boston-bombs.html.

25. Boston police chief wants drones for next year's marathon, RT (Apr. 26, 2013, 16:57), http://rt.com/usa/boston-marathon-surveillance-drones-452/.

26. See, e..g., Radley Balko, ACLU Launches Nationwide Police Militarization Investigation, Huffington Post (Mar. 22, 2013, 12:31 PM EDT), http://www.huffingtonpost.com/2013/03/06/aclu-police-militarization-swat_n_2813334.html; Arthur Rizer & Joseph Hartman, How the War on Terror Has Militarized the Police, Atlantic, Nov. 7, 2011, http://www.theatlantic.com/national/archive/2011/11/how-the-war-on-terror-has-militarized-the-police/248047/.

27. Seattle cancels police drone program after outcry over privacy issues, NBC News (Feb. 8, 2013, 6:39 PM EST), http://usnews.nbcnews.com/_news/2013/02/08/16903237-seattle-cancels-police-drone-program-after-outcry-over-privacy-issues?lite

28. Jason Koebler, City in Virginia Becomes First to Pass Anti-Drone Legislation, US News, Feb. 5, 2013, http://www.usnews.com/news/articles/2013/02/05/city-in-virginia-becomes-first-to-pass-anti-drone-legislation–.

29. Joe Sutton & Catherine E. Shoiche, Florida Gov. Rick Scott signs law restricting drones, CNN (Apr. 26, 2013, 5:42 AM EDT), http://www.cnn.com/2013/04/25/us/florida-drone-law/index.html.

30. An Act to regulate the use of unmanned aerial vehicles, Bill S.1664, available athttp://malegislature.gov/Bills/188/Senate/S1664 (inserting G.L. c. 272, § 99C); see ACLU, The Drone Privacy Act, https://www.aclm.org/drones (last visited May 3, 2013).

31. H.R. 972, 113th Cong. (1st Sess. 2013).

32. H.R. 637, 113th Cong. (1st Sess. 2013)

33. H.R. 1262, 113th Cong. (2d Sess. 2013); see Dave Uberti, Drone makers struggle for acceptance, Bos. Globe, Apr. 6, 2013, http://www.bostonglobe.com/business/2013/04/06/massachusetts-national-drone-companies-are-struggling-gain-public-acceptance-face-controversy/qtCg0CxAIUfrW7applrKWL/story.html("Lawmakers, meanwhile, including Representative Edward Markey of Massachusetts, a candidate for Senate, are introducing legislation to limit how drones can be used by law enforcement, firefighters, farmers, the media, and others in American skies.").

34. See Ryan Delaney, Seeking A 'Field Of Dreams' For A Rising Drone Industry, Nat'l Pub. Radio (Feb. 26, 2013, 3:25 AM), http://www.npr.org/blogs/alltechconsidered/2013/02/26/172883485/seeking-a-field-of-dreams-for-a-rising-drone-industry.

35. Florida v. Riley, 488 U.S. 445, 452 (1989) (O'Connor, J., concurring) ("In my view, the plurality's approach rests the scope of Fourth Amendment protection too heavily on compliance with FAA regulations whose purpose is to promote air safety, not to protect [the right Fourth Amendment right to be free from unreasonable searches]")

36. The Future of Drones in America: Law Enforcement and Privacy Considerations, Sen. Judiciary Comm., Mar. 30, 2013, http://www.judiciary.senate.gov/hearings/hearing.cfmid=d27f2c4073b40a8e678e4a9f6f36acec.

37. See Rosa Brooks, A Drone of One's Own, Foreign Policy, Mar. 21, 2013, http://www.foreignpolicy.com/articles/2013/03/21/a_drone_of_ones_own?page=full.

38. Smart Metric, press release, Global Fingerprint Biometrics Market: $US10 Billion Industry by 2018, Yahoo! Finance (Apr. 11, 2013 11:31 AM EDT), http://finance.yahoo.com/news/global-fingerprint-biometrics-market-us10-153139564.html.

39. Industry: biometrics business valued at $10 billion by 2018, Privacy Matters Blog (Apr. 16, 2013, 15:28), http://privacysos.org/node/1032.

40. See Thom Shanker, To Track Militants, U.S. Has System That Never Forgets a Face, N.Y. Times, July 14, 2011, http://www.nytimes.com/2011/07/14/world/asia/14identity.html?_r=0.

41. See R. Bolle, Guide to Biometrics 81 (2004) (noting facial recognition has inherently high false positive rate).

42. Dan Vergano, Report questions biometric technologies in fighting crime, USA Today, Sept. 27, 2010, http://usatoday30.usatoday.com/tech/news/surveillance/2010-09-27-biometrics27_ST_N.htm.

43. Christopher Bregler, Prof., N.Y.U., interviewed in On The Media, The Future of Surveillence, Apr. 26, 2013, http://www.onthemedia.org/2013/apr/26/future-surveillance/transcript/.

44. 6 U.S.C. § 124h(a). ("The Secretary [of Homeland Security] ...shall establish a Department of Homeland Security State, Local, and Regional Fusion Center Initiative to establish partnerships with State, local, and regional fusion centers.")

45. See Azmat Khan, Senate Report: Massive Post-9/11 Surveillance Apparatus A "Waste", PBS Frontline (Oct.3, 2012, 6:08 PM ET), http://www.pbs.org/wgbh/pages/frontline/iraq-war-on-terror/topsecretamerica/senate-report-massive-post-911-surveillance-apparatus-a-waste/.

46. Investigative Report Criticizes Counterterrorism Reporting, Waste at State & Local Intelligence Fusion Centers, Homeland Sec. & Gov. Affairs Permanent Subcomm. on Investigations, Oct. 3, 2012, http://www.hsgac.senate.gov/subcommittees/investigations/media/investigative-report-criticizes-counterterrorism-reporting-waste-at-state-and-local-intelligence-fusion-centers; see Nancy Murray & Sarah Wunsch,Civil Liberties in Times of Crisis: Lessons from History, 87 Mass. L. Rev. 72, 83 (2002) (warning against sacrificing liberty for security).

47. The Terrorism Delusion, 37 International Security 81, 103 (Summer 2012), available athttp://politicalscience.osu.edu/faculty/jmueller//absisfin.pdf.

48. Dana Priest & William Arkin, Top Secret America 12 (2011).

49. Dana Priest & William Arkin, A hidden world, growing beyond control, Wash. Post. (July 19, 2010 4:50 PM), http://projects.washingtonpost.com/top-secret-america/articles/a-hidden-world-growing-beyond-control/print/.

50. See Michael Kranish, et al., Data-sharing troubles raise questions in Marathon case, Bos. Globe, Apr. 25, 2013, http://www.bostonglobe.com/news/nation/2013/04/24/government-terrorism-information-sharing-program-rated-high-risk-despite-years-effort-since/3ImcHIZOaPKfeeBYTAXRHN/story.html ("A federal audit as recently as January warned there was a 'high risk' that the government's information-communications breakdown allowed the Boston Marathon bomb plot to evolve undetected and its perpetrators to elude quick capture.")

51. Bruce Schneier, Focus on the Threat, N.Y. Times, Room for Debate (Mar. 3, 2010, 7:07 PM), http://roomfordebate.blogs.nytimes.com/2010/05/03/times-square-bombs-and-big-crowds/?src=tptw#bruce.

52. See Ronald Bailey, How Scared of Terrorism Should You Be?, Reason, Sept. 6, 2011, http://reason.com/archives/2011/09/06/how-scared-of-terrorism-should ("chances of being killed by a terrorist are about one in 20 million"); Micah Zenko, Americans Are as Likely to Be Killed by Their Own Furniture as by Terrorism, Atlantic (June 6, 2012, 8:43 AM ET), http://www.theatlantic.com/international/archive/2012/06/americans-are-as-likely-to-be-killed-by-their-own-furniture-as-by-terrorism/258156/ ("For Americans, however, [data on terrorist attacks] should emphasize that an irrational fear of terrorism is both unwarranted and a poor basis for public policy decisions.")

53. See,e.g., Stephen Walt, What Terrorist Threat?, Foreign Policy (Aug. 13, 2012, 12:42 PM), http://walt.foreignpolicy.com/posts/2012/08/13/what_terrorist_threat? ("we continue to over-react to the 'terrorist threat.'"); Fareed Zakaria, What America Has Lost, Newsweek, Sept. 4, 2010, available athttp://www.thedailybeast.com/newsweek/2010/09/04/zakaria-why-america-overreacted-to-9-11.html ("September 11 was a shock to the American psyche and the American system. As a result, we overreacted.")

54. SeeWhitney v. California, 274 U.S. 357, 375 (1927) (Brandeis, J., concurring) ("repression breeds hate; that hate menaces stable government"), overruled byBrandenburg v. Ohio, 395 U.S. 444, 449 (1969).
55. SeeJames Cavallaro, Drones: Killing enemies, and creating them [Blowback], L.A. Times, http://articles.latimes.com/2013/feb/12/news/la-ol-drones-cavallaro-blowback-20130212; see also Spencer Ackerman, Yemeni Tells Senators About 'Fear and Terror' Caused by U.S. Drones,Wired, Danger Room (Apr. 23, 2013, 6:50 PM), http://www.wired.com/dangerroom/2013/04/yemen-drones-muslimi/.
56. Benjamin Wittes & Ritika Singh, James Madison, Presidential Power and Civil Liberties in the War of 1812,in What So Proudly We Hailed 97, 99-100 (Pietro S. Nivola ed. 2012), available at http://www.lawfareblog.com/wp-content/uploads/2012/10/Chapter-5.pdf.
57. Other People's Money (1914), available at http://www.law.louisville.edu/library/collections/brandeis/node/196.
58. See Am. Civil Liberties Union v. C.I.A., 710F.3d 422 (D.C. Cir. 2013).
59. Domestic drones and their unique dangers, Guardian, Mar. 29, 2013, http://www.guardian.co.uk/commentisfree/2013/mar/29/domestic-drones-unique-dangers.
60. See Kyllo v. United States, 533 U.S. 27, 33-34 (2001) ("It would be foolish to contend that the degree of privacy secured to citizens by the Fourth Amendment has been entirely unaffected by the advance of technology."); United States v. Jones, 132 S. Ct. 945, 963 (2012) (Sotomayor, J., concurring) ("The availability and use of these and other new devices will continue to shape the average person's expectations about the privacy of his or her daily movements."); see also Orin S. Kerr, An Equilibrium-Adjustment Theory of the Fourth Amendment, 125 Harv. L. Rev. 476, 514 (2011) (discussing how Brandeis's dissent in Olmstead v. United States, 277 U.S. 438, 478 (1928) and the majority opinion in Katz v. United States, 389 U.S. 347, 353 (1967)were rooted in a reasonable expectation of privacy that underpins the Fourth Amendment).

Drones Can Benefit Civilians and Monitor Human Rights Abuses

Sarah Stein Kerr

Sarah Stein Kerr is a freelance journalist and contributor to Witness.org.

W hat is the first thing that comes to mind when you hear the word "drone?" A predator drone? American foreign policy? Afghanistan, Pakistan, Yemen and the other secret drone strikes unlawfully taking place all over the world? While these concerns are absolutely pressing, there is another important conversation taking place beyond the Obama administration's drone program.

Behind the headlines, policymakers, lawyers, academics, innovators, engineers and aerial robot hobbyists are ruminating upon what some purport as the inevitable; the widespread integration of aerial robots into commerce, service delivery, humanitarian aid, agriculture, environment protection and quite importantly for us at WITNESS, human rights monitoring.

Now before you start rolling your eyes, or writing me off as a crazy Jetsons-loving opportunist, hear me out a little longer. In early October, I had the opportunity to attend the first Drones and Aerial Robotics Conference (DARC) and it got me thinking about a lot of these issues. The purpose of the conference was to bring together professionals from a variety of fields to work on the development of a constructive law and policy agenda for unmanned aerial robots in the United States.

Since then, the Federal Aviation Administration has released extensive guidelines on drone use in American air space. The guidelines will shape our use and perspectives on what is acceptable when it comes to drone use. From a human rights perspective,

"Drones for Good? The Basic Human Rights Considerations," Sarah Stein Kerr, Witness, November 1, 2013, blog.witness.org. Reprinted by permission.

the expansion of the drone market for a wide range of purposes poses a number of challenges surrounding how to ensure that human rights principles are integrated into all potential uses of aerial robots.

Privacy versus security—How to strike a balance when you can see everything?

In January of 2013, the founders of the Genocide Intervention Network wrote an op-ed in the *New York Times* titled "Drones for Human Rights," in which they imagined many possible uses of drones in human rights monitoring and international criminal justice work:

> Drones can reach places and see things cell phones cannot. Social media did not document the worst of the genocide in the remote villages of Darfur in 2003 and 2004. Camera-toting protesters could not enter the fields where 8,000 men and boys were massacred in Srebrenica in 1995. Graphic and detailed evidence of crimes against humanity does not guarantee a just response, but it helps.

The piece yielded a wave of responses, with many correctly arguing that it did not touch upon many other human rights-related issues that would arise from a sky filled with drones or a sky with just one single surveillance drone.

While the possibilities are exciting, a wealth of thought must be invested in considering how drones could be used to capture evidence of human rights violations without also violating our human right to privacy. This is obviously a tricky balance to strike when dealing with aerial photography, since you never know exactly what or who you are going to capture on film.

Other questions that immediately arise include: who should be allowed to use drones for human rights purposes? Could drones actually be used for international human rights monitoring given their use would involve violating a nation's airspace? With no national or international framework for these types of activities, it is important that the human rights community begin to engage governments and civil society actors with some of the big questions surrounding this new frontier.

Values and design: Is it possible to build a "drone for good?"

In considering the possibility of drones for human rights monitoring another important step is imagining the potential components and functionalities of a "drone for good." In the tech world, there are many who believe that in its individual components, technology is value neutral and as creators we instill our values in technology as we design and build it.

This perspective poses a key question; how do you build an aerial robot that operationalizes key human rights values such as privacy, security, safety, freedom of expression and respect? How do we work to make sure that it stays in the right hands and is equipped with capabilities that have the potential to actually protect human lives (such as video cameras that produce media with extensive metadata that can be securely sent via email)?

Some would argue that this idea of embedding values in technology is not actually possible because some technologies are inherently valued in their overarching functionalities. For example with a drone, even the act of creating something that flies or looms over individuals allots power in the hand of one actor without the consultation of the other, which can be seen as an expression of values in itself. This is also a critical dimension of this discussion that must be considered.

Intrigued? Mildly terrified? Want to learn more?

Good. Moving forward, it is crucial that we examine the opportunities presented by this technology but also strongly scrutinize the limitations and possible effects of more widespread use. And the time to start thinking is now. The initial rules are being written and the human rights community (and many other actors) must be prepared to contribute substantive policy suggestions to support the protection of human rights and safety of individuals across the globe.

Domestic Non-Military Drones Are Here to Stay

Deirdre Fulton

Deirdre Fulton is a Common Dreams staff writer.

D omestic non-military drone use took one step closer to widespread implementation on Sunday, as the Federal Aviation Administration issued proposed regulations for small, unmanned aircraft systems in the U.S.

According to an FAA press release, the rule would limit flights to daylight and visual-line-of-sight operations. It also addresses height restrictions, operator certification, aircraft registration and marking, and operational limits. In a blow to Google and Amazon, it does not permit drone delivery.

Also on Sunday, the White House issued an Executive Order requiring every federal agency to develop "a framework regarding privacy, accountability, and transparency for commercial and private [Unmanned Aircraft Systems] use" within 90 days and with an eye toward protecting personal privacy, civil rights, and civil liberties.

"Together, the FAA regulations and the White House order provide some basic rules of the sky that will govern who can fly drones in the United States and under what conditions, while attempting to prevent aviation disasters and unrestrained government surveillance," the *Washington Post* declared.

But civil liberties experts warned that the FAA rules and presidential memo leave the door open for invasions of privacy by the government and corporations.

"Surveillance, Privacy Concerns Raised as FAA Gives Domestic Drones a Nod," Deirdre Fulton, Common Dreams, February 15, 2015. http://www.commondreams.org/news/2015/02/15/surveillance-privacy-concerns-raised-faa-gives-domestic-drones-nod. Licensed under CC BY SA 3.0.

"The proposed rules do absolutely nothing to address privacy, except perhaps require some identifying markings displayed in the 'largest practicable manner' such that you may be able to identify who owns the drone that is spying on you," Ryan Calo wrote at Forbes. "I was on the conference call announcing the new rules and the Secretary of Transportation mentioned the importance of privacy and civil liberties, but this commitment is not reflected in the proposed rules."

The Center for Democracy and Technology called on Congress to raise the bar on domestic drone standards.

"Drones have the potential for significant societal, scientific, and economic benefits, but also pose new and intrusive privacy problems," CDT senior counsel Harley Geiger said in a press statement. "The White House's memo requires government agencies to enhance transparency and develop clear rules to protect the privacy of Americans. This is an important and welcome step in advancing drone technology, while protecting civil liberties."

Still, he added, "the White House memo itself does not establish strong privacy and transparency drone standards for agencies, leaving it up to the agencies to develop these standards. Because the memo's requirements are not specific, the drone policies the agencies set for themselves will be key to how individuals' privacy is actually protected. Congress still has a role to play in setting strong privacy and transparency standards for drone use."

One of the most promising applications for domestic drone use is also one of the most troubling: as an internet service platform, giving operators access to vast quantities of data and threatening net neutrality, Drew Mitnick and Jack Bussell note at the blog for Access, a global human rights organization focused on digital freedom.

"Drones also increase the opportunities for governments to conduct first-hand surveillance of users' electronic communications by intercepting signals and information," they write. "Official documents demonstrate that government agencies are already exploring aerial platforms for surveillance technologies, like

Stingray technology, which conducts bulk surveillance of user location information...The potential for drones to violate individual rights supports the need for legislation and regulations for government uses of drones as well as commercial vehicles."

Mitnick and Bussell continue:

> Drones provide great capacity to benefit both users and industry. However, drone technology is still new, and it will likely be utilized in ways we cannot imagine today. Access hopes that the process initiated by the Obama Administration will provide clear, lasting rules for drone use, particularly for use as an internet service platform, both in a pseudo-permanent and temporary capacity, and the rules that these providers must abide by, including issues of network neutrality. By addressing hard questions now, we can provide for a path forward that allows for innovation without sacrificing user rights.

According to the Post, "the FAA and the White House had intended to unveil their new drone rules later this month. But an official document highlighting some of the proposed regulations was inadvertently posted on a federal Web site Friday night, prompting the Obama administration to announce the changes in the middle of a holiday weekend."

Domestic Drones Violate Fourth Amendment Rights

Rand Paul

Randal Howard "Rand" Paul is an American politician and physician. Since 2011, Paul has served in the United States Senate as a member of the Republican Party representing Kentucky.

When assuming office, every government official must take an oath to abide by and uphold our Constitution. Since 2010, I have made that my mission in Congress. Unfortunately, the Obama administration is not upholding nor abiding by the Constitution—in fact, this administration is going to great lengths to continually violate it.

Its most recent transgression involves the use of domestic drones.

These small drones are to be used as a crime fighting tool for law enforcement officials. But is unwarranted and constant surveillance by an aerial eye of Big Government the answer?

In a memorandum issued by President Barack Obama's secretary of the Air Force, the stated purpose of these drones is "balancing ... obtaining intelligence information ... and protecting individual rights guaranteed by the U.S. Constitution."

However, flying over our homes, farms, ranches and businesses and spying on us while we conduct our everyday lives is not an example of protecting our rights. It is an example of violating them.

The domestic use of drones to spy on Americans clearly violates the Fourth Amendment and limits our rights to personal privacy. I do not want a drone hovering over my house, taking photos of whether I separate my recyclables from my garbage.

When I have friends over for a barbecue, the government drone is not on the invitation list. I do not want a drone monitoring where I go, what I do and for how long I do whatever it is that I'm doing. I do not want a nanny state watching over my every move.

We should not be treated like criminals or terrorists while we are simply conducting our everyday lives. We should not have our rights infringed upon by unwarranted police-state tactics.

I have introduced legislation into the Senate that restates the Constitution.

This bill protects individual privacy against unwarranted governmental intrusion through the use of these drones. The Preserving Freedom from Unwarranted Surveillance Act of 2012 will protect Americans' personal privacy by forcing the government to honor our Fourth Amendment rights.

I want to make it clear that I am not arguing against the use of technology. But like other tools used to collect information in law enforcement, a warrant needs to be issued to use drones domestically. The police force should have the power to collect intelligence; however, I believe they must go through a judge and request a warrant to do so. The judicial branch must have some authority over drones, as they do with other law enforcement tools.

My bill will restate the Fourth Amendment and protect American's privacy by forcing police officials to obtain a warrant before using domestic drones.

There are some exceptions within this bill, such as the patrol of our national borders, when immediate action is needed to prevent "imminent danger to life," and when we are under a high risk of a terrorist attack. Otherwise, the government must have probable cause that led them to ask for a warrant before the use of drones is permitted.

If the warrant is not obtained, this act would allow any person to sue the government. This act also specifies that no evidence obtained or collected in violation of this act can be admissible as evidence in a criminal, civil or regulatory action.

Allowing domestic drones to act as spies for the government is a complete violation of our basic right to personal privacy.

Unrestricted drone surveillance conjures up images reminiscent of Orwell's "1984"—a totalitarian police-state. According to the Fourth Amendment, "The right of the people to be secure in their persons, houses, papers and effects, against unreasonable searches and seizures, shall not be violated."

I am sure our police force had good intentions with their suggested drone policies, but do they understand the consequences? Do they realize that they are allowing the government to act as the eye in the sky?

By infringing upon our rights and watching over our every move, the government is not going to protect us, but they will push us one more step closer to completely losing our Fourth Amendment rights. My bill will protect individual privacy against governmental intrusion by these drones and establish a balance by requiring judicial action and allowing protection in court.

I am confident that my colleagues in the Senate will agree with this bill. Each and every one of us took the same oath to abide by and uphold our Constitution. The Preserving Freedom from Unwarranted Surveillance Act does just that.

We Need Regulations for Commercial Drones

Konstantin Kakaes

Konstantin Kakaes is a program fellow with the international security program at New America.

Cyclone Pam tore through Vanuatu in the South Pacific in March 2015, destroying or damaging 17,000 buildings and displacing 65,000 people from their homes. Shortly after the storm, humanitarian first responders and journalists began flying drones over the affected area to document the devastation.

Drones have become an increasingly important tool for quick, comprehensive damage assessment after natural disasters, but such footage can be invasive. As Matt Waite, who runs the Drone Journalism Lab at the University of Nebraska, points out, "a lot of these houses had their roofs ripped off but the walls still intact." In video NBC news shot after the storm, you can clearly see inside. "What if newlyweds decided to do what newlyweds do at that particular moment you happen to be flying along?" Waite asks.

Many in the humanitarian community have adopted a voluntary code of conduct that lays out some guidelines about how to fly drones safely and gather information in a way that respects people's privacy. But there is no such code of conduct for the growing number of private and commercial entities that use drones, including news outlets, which are resisting even non-binding guidelines that might restrict access to the air.

Here's why we need such guidelines: Legal scholars argue that airspace is neither wholly private nor wholly public, but something in between. By resisting any privacy safeguards in this nebulous space, media organizations and their representatives may be facilitating massive violations of privacy by large corporations under the guise of protecting free speech.

"Drones Can Photograph Almost Anything. But Should They?" Konstantin Kakaes, *Columbia Journalism Review*, April 21, 2016. Reprinted with permission.

Concepts like privacy, nuisance, and trespassing are defined in common law—the accumulation of court decisions over decades—as opposed to laws passed by Congress. In coming years, courts will define and interpret these concepts in a world full of drones. But courts can, at best, figure out what is legal and illegal; they aren't equipped to restrain what might be technically legal but ill-advised. Voluntary guidelines can protect privacy in a way that courts can't—and vice versa.

Just over a year ago, President Barack Obama called on interested members of the public to collaboratively "develop and communicate best practices for privacy, accountability, and transparency" as they relate to drone use. The goal is to come up with guidelines for commercial and private drone operators that would allow the budding unmanned aerial vehicle industry to develop while also preserving the right to privacy—something like what the humanitarian community has already done, but for all non-governmental drone users.

Obama put an agency of the Department of Commerce called the National Telecommunications and Information Administration, known as the NTIA, in charge of organizing the process. The NTIA is not supposed to write the guidelines itself, but only to nudge participants toward consensus. The Federal Aviation Administration (FAA) is the agency that has authority to make binding rules about who can fly where, and Congress is currently debating a new law that will revamp what the FAA is supposed to do with respect to drones and more generally. The Senate passed a version of the bill this week that sets a mid-2016 deadline for completion of the NTIA process.

Meanwhile, a quiet battle between the First and Fourth Amendments has been unfolding in a Washington conference room, pitting news organizations that want unfettered access to the view from the air against privacy advocates and even lobbyists for big technology companies, who want at least some rules to keep drones out of people's personal lives.

The NTIA group has met five times, and has scheduled a sixth meeting for mid-May, at which participants hope to agree to a finalized set of guidelines. A previous NTIA-mediated attempt to come up with guidelines for the use of facial recognition software broke down last year when the Electronic Frontier Foundation, the American Civil Liberties Union (ACLU), and other groups walked out, in protest that "companies wouldn't even agree to the most modest measures to protect privacy." This time around, it is lobbyists for media companies who have the strongest objections to guidelines that would protect privacy. "We have a real problem with privacy rights groups trying to say that you have a privacy right when you are out in public," says Mickey Osterreicher, general counsel of the National Press Photographers Association.

For news organizations, the rationale for not restricting drone use is simple. "You don't need a person's permission to photograph them when they are out in public," says Osterreicher. The rules should not be any different, he says, if a photographer is using a camera attached to a drone: "We should not be creating new laws based solely on the fact that it involves a new technology."

Even voluntary standards can be problematic, some media representatives say. A company can be sued for not following such standards, even if it never agreed to them, warns Chuck Tobin, a partner at Holland & Knight, a DC lobbying firm that represents a large coalition of media companies, including The Washington Post, The New York Times, the Associated Press, Thomson Reuters, NBC, ABC, and Advance Publications.

Tobin and Osterreicher argue that there shouldn't be any privacy-related restraints on drone use in public, while in private spaces, drone operators should pay attention to their subjects' "reasonable expectation of privacy." But this laissez-faire approach is bad for the newspapers and magazines they represent, and for the public at large.

The First Amendment protects information-gathering because it guarantees both freedom of speech generally and freedom of the press in particular. If I'm not allowed to take a picture, according to a 2012 decision by a Federal appeals court in Chicago, then I can't exercise my free speech right by publishing it, so a restraint on picture-taking is a restraint on speech. The same logic applies to the freedom of the press. However, as the Supreme Court found in a 1965 case, "the right to speak and publish does not carry with it an unrestrained right to gather information."

Our skies are filling with cameras. The American public bought almost a million drones in 2015. The millions of drones in private hands are being joined by tens of thousands flown by corporations. Some companies, like Amazon and Google, plan ambitious national drone delivery networks. This means that, in much of the country, a drone owned by one of those mega-companies may soon be overhead almost constantly, on its way to your neighbor's house to deliver a package.

Any commercial drone flight requires a special FAA exemption. Almost 5,000 such exemptions have been issued as of April 18, of which just over 200 mention newsgathering as at least one of their missions. Additionally, after a year of lobbying by media lawyers, the FAA announced in May 2015 that journalistic organizations may use drone footage or images recorded by third parties without such an exemption. The only restriction is that the journalist must not have had "operational control" of the drone.

The proliferation of drones will change American day-to-day life in profound ways. Drones are increasingly able to loiter indefinitely overhead, and to photograph events in the murky boundary between private and public space. Take, for instance, a movie set. Actors in last year's Star Wars reboot wore heavy robes over their costumes and hid their faces as they walked from movie trailers to the set, Waite notes, because paparazzi were using drones to snap pictures of the actors. Producers reportedly resorted to hiring their own teams of counter-drone drone operators.

For all the promise of drone journalism, there are relatively few examples of drones having been used in the US in a journalistically noteworthy way. This is partly because the FAA still makes it relatively difficult to get permission to fly. But it might also be because their significance for journalism has been exaggerated. Tobin, the media lobbyist, cites a New York Times video from Greenland, TV footage of a frozen Niagara falls, a CNN video taken in Selma, Alabama, and footage taken after a tornado. All of these are nice enough, but none is transformative. There's every reason to believe drones will become only a useful niche tool for journalism—a new sort of telephoto lens.

The arrival of hundreds of thousands of drones is, of course, not an isolated phenomenon. The sky isn't the only place filling with cameras. CCTV cameras on street corners in major cities, wearable cameras, and cameras on mobile phones are changing the nature of privacy. Clear-cut cases in which a drone, say, loiters outside someone's bedroom window, are indeed easily resolved with existing common law precedents against trespassing, nuisance, and harassment. But what about examples that aren't so obvious, like using a drone with a telephoto lens flying hundreds of feet in the air to surreptitiously take pictures of protesters at a demonstration? "Our general rubric," Tobin says, "is if it's in a public place, and the public can see it, the public has a First Amendment right to record it and disseminate it to other people."

Tobin's view puts him at odds with legal scholars and some Supreme Court justices. As the film set example points out, there are many instances in which a drone's capabilities can enable it to infringe on privacy in novel ways. Because the constitutional protections for information-gathering are implicit rather than explicit, different Federal courts have drawn the line in different places, and scholars and judges disagree about how strong the protections are. As a result, according to an article in the William and Mary Law Review, there is "considerable uncertainty over First Amendment protection of information-gathering."

In a recent and widely-cited opinion, Justice Sonia Sotomayor made the point that recording and aggregating the history of movements even in public, "enables the Government to ascertain, more or less at will, [people's] political and religious beliefs, sexual habits, and so on." Though individual data points, such as my presence on a particular street corner at a particular time, might be perfectly innocuous, she asked, is the same true of a compilation of everywhere I've been today, or over the last week or month?

A recent report by the Congressional Research Service pointed out that government agencies can't use drones for domestic surveillance unless they figure out the Fourth Amendment implications. Technically, the Fourth Amendment doesn't affect what private citizens or companies can do with drones (or anything else). It only applies to searches (and seizures) by government agencies. But as the William and Mary law review article points out, "It will be hard for people to argue that they are unsettled and made insecure by police drone use in a world where they expect—and have adapted to—being subject to drone surveillance by everyone else." This means that if we want Fourth Amendment protection against police use of drones, we might also have to accept some limits on what other people, including journalists, do with drones.

This doesn't, as the William and Mary law review article says, mean doing away with the First Amendment. It just means balancing two elements of the Bill of Rights. Privacy rights, the article argues, should depend on what type of recording is being made (for instance, whether it's a video recorded by a surveillance camera or a work of art); who is recording (a credentialed journalist or a marketing company); what the recording is about (is it a matter of public interest?); and whether the government's restriction is intended to muzzle speech (by, say, giving preferential privacy protections to a company that has political influence). None of these distinctions is necessarily clear cut, but these are sensible questions to ask.

Take, for instance, the case of William Meredith and John David Boggs of Bullitt County, Kentucky, south of Louisville. Boggs was flying a drone, a common consumer model, and Meredith shot it down with a shotgun. Meredith was charged with criminal mischief and wanton endangerment, but a local judge dismissed the charges, ruling that the drone was flying low enough to violate Meredith's privacy, based on eyewitness testimony. Boggs, though, released video to news outlets that appears to show he was flying much higher than Meredith said he was, and therefore wouldn't have been able to effectively spy on Meredith (who he calls the "drone slayer").

In January, Boggs sued Meredith for destruction of property. The courts will likely take years to definitively resolve their case. In late March, an Arkansas man shot down a drone with a rifle because, he told police, he feared the drone was taking pictures of his kids, who were jumping on a trampoline in the backyard. Rather than waiting for the courts, it makes sense to craft guidelines that proactively parse difficult territory and balance conflicting rights.

The process Obama set in motion last year has been underway since August, culminating with the NTIA's most recent meeting in Washington in late February, when Tobin and his colleagues proposed a set of guidelines that give commercial drone operators carte blanche to write rules for themselves. According to the Holland & Knight guidelines, commercial drone operators "should be guided by the standards and practices of the organizations for which they work," both in how they use drones and in how they use the data drones gather. If that organization has well-thought-out standards and practices, this works out swimmingly. But what if it doesn't? What if that organization, instead of being a civic-minded newspaper, is a gossip website, or a shady marketing company?

Tobin says he and his colleagues "became reluctant craftspeople." They "put pen to paper," he says, because other drafts that had circulated at the NTIA meetings gave insufficient attention to the First Amendment. Other groups, including the Center for Democracy and Technology (CDT), an advocacy group, and Hogan Lovells, a law firm whose clients include the National Association of Broadcasters, have been trying to write a consensus draft. (Disclosure: I have been present at the NTIA meetings as an interested observer and participant, and have given comments to both CDT and Hogan Lovells on their drafts, as well as to lawyers working for Amazon who have combined the two drafts.) That consensus calls for drone operators to "avoid knowingly retain[ing] personal data longer than reasonably necessary to fulfill the purpose for which the data were collected."

This means journalists who want to can, within the guidelines, keep pictures for as long as they think they need to, but that if an Amazon delivery drone films everything it sees while delivering a package, Amazon should delete that footage after the package is successfully delivered. Tobin says guidelines like these infringe on the First Amendment. "To us, the First Amendment is a foundational principle," he says.

To understand what the non-binding guidelines might look like, it's helpful to think of Google's Street View. Google's cameras take pictures of people, cars, and the fronts of buildings in what are clearly public spaces. But Google voluntarily blurs the faces of individuals and the license plates of vehicles because these constitute "personally identifiable information." Some still see Street View as an invasion of privacy, but blurring mitigates the privacy harm, even if Google has the right under the First Amendment to take such pictures. This type of voluntary redaction is a good idea. It doesn't make Street View any less useful for its intended purpose of helping people navigate, and it makes it a little less intrusive. It doesn't eliminate unintended privacy consequences: even though his face was blurred, this guy's wife still famously caught him sneaking a cigarette in a Street View picture.

Data retention in the context of journalism can be a tricky question. As Holland & Knight point out in an NTIA filing, pictures of O.J. Simpson taken in 1993 were used in his trial years later to "show that he owned Bruno Magli shoes that he claimed he never owned." That is one reason the CDT-Hogan Lovells draft doesn't place hard restrictions on how long data should be retained. It just points out that it's worth thinking carefully about whether data ought to be retained.

The Hogan Lovells-CDT draft, put together by a loose coalition of industry representatives and privacy advocates, tries to place voluntary limits on the use of persistent surveillance drones for marketing, or say, credit or health care treatment eligibility. The best practices are voluntary, and liberally sprinkled with caveats. As in the Street View example, they call for drone operators to avoid displaying data unless it is necessary to the task at hand. But it doesn't prohibit them from doing so, it just says that they should make a "reasonable" effort to blur images.

Similarly, it calls on commercial operators to make "reasonable" efforts to protect personal data from hackers. It says that unless there is a "compelling need," drones shouldn't be used to gather data for monitoring people's eligibility for "employment, credit, or health care treatment." For example, your health insurance company should be discouraged (though not prohibited) from monitoring your exercise habits—did you really go running by the lake this morning?—using a drone.

By contrast, the Holland & Knight document proposes that, "[i]n public spaces, UAS operators may use UAS without limitations to capture data or images as with any other technology. There shall be no limitations or restrictions on the subsequent use of data or images gathered by UAS in public spaces." In plain terms, this means that if you are in public, Holland & Knight think anyone has the right to use a drone to keep track of where you are going, and where you have been, for any length of time.

Waite, the journalism professor, was one of the first people to use drones for journalistic purposes in the US, and hopes to continue doing so. "I have no interest in the government getting involved in speech issues," he says. Even if some media outlets "take their First Amendment missions seriously…and try to do this the right way," others use the First Amendment only nominally, as a tool to push the boundaries in pursuit of profit. Voluntary guidelines that seek to balance privacy and the right to gather information are reasonable, Waite says.

Balancing the right to gather information with the right to privacy has never been easy. New technologies for image and data gathering and analysis, like drones and facial and voice recognition software, make finding the balance even harder, in part because such innovations change what is realistically possible. In the past, the high cost of, say, loitering in front of someone's door for weeks at a time and filming video the whole time would have made it effectively impossible for journalists and law enforcement to do what a drone will be able to do very cheaply in the near future. Tobin says that just as people got used to film cameras in the late 19th century, they should, and will, get used to "perpetual surveillance" today.

In 1890, Louis Brandeis and Samuel Warren published a landmark essay called The Right to Privacy. "The intensity and complexity of life, attendant upon advancing civilization, have rendered necessary some retreat from the world, and man, under the refining influence of culture, has become more sensitive to publicity, so that solitude and privacy have become more essential to the individual," they wrote.

Solitude and privacy are at least as important to journalists themselves as they are to the public at large. As the William and Mary law review article says, "the First Amendment itself is arguably conflicted as greater recording leads to greater amounts of expression, but can chill freedoms of association and personal development that make for meaningful expression and deliberative participation." Their arguments echo those of Julie Cohen of Georgetown University Law Center, who has pointed out that privacy shapes the structure of our economy and society in subtle, but vital ways, and that as privacy is diminished, democracy is threatened.

Despite growing recognition of the importance of privacy, with drones as with other technologies, privacy violations that might seem unwise to most people will be allowed by law. Just because you can fly over someone's ruined house and film them inside it, should you?

Voluntary guidelines can hardly solve all the dilemmas provoked by the "intensity and complexity" of modern technology, but they can be a start. It may well be that this attempt to find a consensus will fail as the previous NTIA process around facial recognition did. That would be a loss for the public at large, and for journalists in particular.

CHAPTER 4

Are Civilian Drones a Danger to Society?

Overview: A Look at Domestic Drones in the United States

Simone Richmond

Simone Richmond is a journalist and grant writer.

I n recent months, the United States' policy of drone attacks to kill suspected militants in Pakistan, Afghanistan, Somalia, Libya and Yemen has come under heated criticism. The extrajudicial targeted killings of suspects, including American citizens, is in itself a stark violation of international law. Add to that the fact that President Obama has ordered hundreds of strikes (over five times as many so far as did his predecessor Bush) and the indiscriminate slaughter of civilians (now estimated at over a thousand by the most conservative estimates) with drones' missiles inevitably raining down on funeral gatherings and mosques; the posthumous classification of all military-age male casualties as "militants" for the purposes of P.R.; and the creepy image of Obama fretting over the biography of each suspect on his "kill list."

With their courageous acts of civil disobedience at the Air Force and Air National Guard bases that control the drone strikes, Code Pink and other activist groups are sounding the clarion call that these remote-controlled killers commit war crimes. But amidst the growing recognition of the brutal effects of armed drones abroad, it's also time for activists to take a hard look at the brave new world of surveillance drones being used here in the United States.

In February, Congress quietly passed a bill that enables the Federal Aviation Administration (FAA) to fast-track the "efficient integration" of Unmanned Aerial Vehicles (UAVs) into the national airspace, with nary a cost-benefit analysis or impact study. This came after the December crash of a U.S. drone on the Iranian border, which highlighted both the high crash rates of drones and the windfall of intelligence that the vulnerabilities of U.S. stealth technology could reveal to its stated enemies. The bill also lacks mention of privacy risk assessment or protection, to the alarm of civil liberties advocates. Since its passage, a number of citizen groups—the ACLU, Electronic Freedom Foundation, the Electronic Privacy Information Center, a congressional caucus led by Ed Markey (D-Mass) & Joe Barton (R-TX)—have been calling on Congress to address the "invasive and pervasive surveillance" that it makes inevitable, but to no avail.

Barring passage of stricter regulations, it seems government and private surveillance drones are poised to enter already crowded skies. As it stands, the FAA currently authorizes 20 state and local governments and 24 universities and other entities, including police departments from Utah to Arkansas, to fly airborne surveillance devices. In May, the chief deputy of the Montgomery County, Texas, sheriff's office told a newspaper that his department plans to deploy rubber bullets and tear gas from its drone, on which he also hopes to mount Tazers and beanbag cannons. (With $300,000 of federal Homeland Security grant funds, his department made headlines when it prepared to become the first police agency in the U.S. to order a drone that could carry weapons.)

In the profligate world of defense contracts, drone research and development are going strong, bringing us ever closer to the Clinton-era Department of Defense's "Joint Vision 2020," which imagined the U.S. at the helm of a ring of satellites girding the earth, combining all-seeing vision with deadly force. In March, two drones performed the first-ever successful test of autonomous in-flight refueling at 45,000 feet, and it was revealed that Sandia National Labs & Northrup have favorably assessed the feasibility of a nuclear-powered drone. Two months later, NATO capped off its summit by signing a $1.7 billion deal with Northrup Grumman for its Global Hawk UAVs to be integrated into NATO's "Allied Ground Surveillance" system. On June 1, a liquid hydrogen-fueled

Boeing spy drone called "Phantom Eye," designed to stay aloft for four or more days at a time, completed a successful flight.

It's not news that the U.S. spends vast sums on shiny new toys for the military while its municipal budgets are strapped. What's startling is that both trends may well yield more drones. While critics of runaway military spending, waste and fraud can credibly point to the unwieldy cost of military drones—in March, the Air Force assessed the cost of an unexplained August 2011 drone crash in Afghanistan to be $72.8 million—the future of domestic surveillance drones, in contrast, appears shockingly inexpensive.

"The drones cost $3.36 an hour to operate, which compares to $250 to $600 an hour for a manned aircraft," a county policeman from Denver told Bloomberg. "Governments that in the past couldn't afford helicopters can now afford UAVs," explained the spokesman for a defense-industry consulting firm. Now, for about the cost of a squad car, a local police department can get a drone.

Should city and county governments nationwide wish to look to drone surveillance as the answer to their budget problem and not know where to turn, the federal government is ready to help. In May, The Department of Homeland Security launched its Air-Based Technologies Program, which will "facilitate and accelerate the adoption" of small, unmanned drones by police and other public safety agencies, positioning DHS as the central point of coordination for private aviation technology manufacturers and police and sheriffs departments nationwide. DHS already runs the nation's largest fleet of domestic surveillance drones: the Customs and Border Protection Agency has used them to monitor U.S. borders for illegal immigration and drugs since 2005, at a cost of more than $250 million to date, with unimpressive results toward its stated intent. Nonetheless, Homeland Security's drone program will continue to be well-endowed, and by 2016 it will have the ability to deploy a drone anywhere in domestic airspace within three hours' time.

The image conjured of a militarized, federally-coordinated surveillance state is augured by the preparations now underway for the 2012 London Olympics. London's security system will include surface-to-air missile systems, supplemented by drones and coordinated with checkpoints, ground-level scanners, biometric ID cards, and license plate and facial-recognition CCTV systems. In Athens, site of the 2004 Olympics, the police evidently intended to keep the surveillance and security systems in place when the games were finished, and it would seem that only the rampant corruption, poor management and faulty implementation that plagued the system in the first place prevented police from using it to quash protests earlier this year.

Given that the deployment of these surveillance drones is in the works, activists must begin to develop strategies for confronting such a surveillance state, including possibilities for allying or actively collaborating with nontraditional allies across traditional political lines. At one end of the political spectrum, the movement for transparency and oversight is anchored by liberal civil-liberties stalwarts like the ACLU and the Electronic Frontier Foundation, which recently obtained via FOIA request the list of 50 organizations already legally flying drones.

Meanwhile, the topic of domestic drones has recently captured the conservative imagination. In June, when a Twitter user's misinterpretation of a Fox News story led to a widespread false rumor that the Environmental Protection Agency was using drones to spy on farmers suspected of polluting the water supply, it took only a few days for the story to gain speed, amplified by conservative blogs such as NetRightDaily, then erroneously repeated by Fox News and other outlets; at least four Republican congressmen were demanding answers from the EPA before the story was dispelled.

The fact that such a prospect (true or not) provoked such outrage on the right provides a powerful lesson. Working together across political lines, activists could more powerfully assert the demand for privacy and accountability—perhaps even take advantage of the existing lax legislation to create DIY robotics to aid in acts of civil disobedience, reporting or art. While all who are concerned about human rights are surely grateful for activists and reporters focusing in on war crimes by U.S. robots of war abroad, let it not distract us from organizing and strategizing around the less deadly but more insidious specter of the surveillance state at home that, if left unchecked, will soon be set in motion.

Concerns About Drone Safety Yield an Unpopular Solution

Kevin Poulsen

Kevin Poulsen is a contributing editor at Wired, *a former black-hat hacker, and author of* Kingpin: How One Hacker Took Over the Billion-Dollar Cybercrime Underground.

I f you want to understand why the government freaked out when a $400 remote-controlled quadcopter landed on the White House grounds last week, you need to look four miles away, to a small briefing room in Arlington, Virginia. There, just 10 days earlier, officials from the US military, the Department of Homeland Security, and the FAA gathered for a DHS "summit" on a danger that had been consuming them privately for years: the potential use of hobbyist drones as weapons of terror or assassination.

The conference was open to civilians, but explicitly closed to the press. One attendee described it as an eye-opener. The officials played videos of low-cost drones firing semi-automatic weapons, revealed that Syrian rebels are importing consumer-grade drones to launch attacks, and flashed photos from an exercise that pitted $5,000 worth of drones against a convoy of armored vehicles. (The drones won.) But the most striking visual aid was on an exhibit table outside the auditorium, where a buffet of low-cost drones had been converted into simulated flying bombs. One quadcopter, strapped to 3 pounds of inert explosive, was a DJI Phantom 2, a newer version of the very drone that would land at the White House the next week.

Attendee Daniel Herbert snapped a photo and posted it to his website along with detailed notes from the conference. The day after the White House incident, he says, DHS phoned him and politely asked him to remove the entire post. He complied. "I'm

"Why the US Government Is Terrified of Hobbyist Drones," Kevin Poulsen, *Wired*, February 5, 2015. Reprinted by permission.

not going to be the one to challenge Homeland Security and cause more contention," says Herbert, who runs a small drone shop in Delaware called Skygear Solutions.

The White House drone, of course, wasn't packing an explosive and wasn't piloted by a terrorist—just a Washingtonian who lost control of the device while playing around in the wee hours. But the gentle censorship directed at Herbert illustrates how serious the issue is to counterterrorism officials.

A Drone Maker Takes Decisive Action

The Phantom line of consumer drones made by China-based DJI figures prominently in the government's attack scenarios. That's not because there's anything sinister about DJI or the Phantom—in fact, just the opposite. The Phantom is the iPod of drones, cheap, easy to use, and as popular with casual and first-time fliers as with experienced radio control enthusiasts.

With all the attention surrounding the White House landing, DJI felt it had to take action. So last Thursday it pushed a "mandatory firmware update" for its Phantom 2 that would prevent the drone from flying in a 15.5 mile radius of the White House. So far it's the only drone-maker installing what's known as GPS geofencing

The technique is not new to DJI. The company first added no-fly zones to its firmware in April of last year to deter newbie pilots from zipping into the restricted airspace over airports, where they might interfere with departing and arriving aircraft. If a Phantom 2 pilot flies within five miles of a major airport's no fly zone, the drone's maximum altitude begins to taper. At 1.5 miles away, it lands and refuses to take off again. Municipal airports are protected by smaller zones, also programmed into the drones' firmware.

For DJI, airport no-fly zones were a response to the growing popularity of the Phantom 2 and perhaps a hedge against the constant threat of increased regulation. "We started seeing the community of pilots grow," says spokesman Michael Perry, and many users have no idea where they can and can't legally fly the drone. "The guy in the White House incident, I'm pretty sure he didn't know that flying in downtown DC is illegal." Rather than put the onus on every user to learn local air traffic zoning rules, DJI translated them into code, and added a little buffer zone of its own for added safety.

The White House geofence is only the second one that isn't centered on an airport, according to Perry—the first was Tiananmen Square. It won't be the last. Now that the company has perfected the ability to erect geofences at will, the sky's the limit—or, more accurately, the skies are limited. DJI is preparing an update that will increase the number of airport no fly zones from 710 to 10,000, and prevent users from flying across some national borders—a reaction to the recent discovery that drug smugglers are trying to use drones to fly small loads of meth from Mexico into the US.

"I Want to Fly Wherever the Heck I Want"

This geofencing has critics, including hobbyists chagrined to find their favorite flying spot suddenly encompassed by DJI no-fly zones. "I live just inside a red zone and find it quite offensive that a company would attempt to restrict any potential usage in/around my own house," one user wrote in response to the first geofencing update last April.

"One could theorize that every zone anywhere could be a restricted zone," wrote another. "Thank you but no thank you. If I spend thousands of dollars then I want to fly wherever the heck I want as long as it is under 400ft and 500ft away from airports."

"This is NOT something users want," another critic added. "I have a good relationship with my local airports and have worked with every local tower or control center. I get clearance to fly and they have been great, but this 'update' takes away my control."

Ryan Calo, a University of Washington law professor who studies robots and the law, traces the resistance to two sources. "One is a complaint about restricting innovation. The second one says you should own your own stuff, and it's a liberty issue: corporate verses individual control and autonomy," Calo says.

"When I purchase something I own it, and when someone else controls what I own, it will be serving someone else's interest, not mine."

DJI, in other words, has flown into one a core discontent of the Internet age. Technology's no-fly zones already are everywhere. Lexmark printers and Keurig coffee makers have been programmed to reject third-party ink cartridges and coffee pods. Auto dealers are beginning to install remote-control immobilizers in cars sold to sub-prime borrowers, so they can shut down a driver who's delinquent with an auto payment (the technology already has resulted in a 100-vehicle automotive hack attack.) In 2009, some Kindle owners discovered Amazon has the power to remotely delete the book they're reading, after the company purged George Orwell's *1984* and *Animal Farm* from e-book readers, an action Jeff Bezos later apologized for.

"The fate of small drone flights over DC may seem like a little thing—a spat worked out among private players," wrote EFF's Parker Higgins in a blog post Monday. "But these small battles shape the notion of what it means to own something and illustrate the growing control of manufacturers over user conduct."

Geofencing Won't Prevent Terrorism

While alarming to some, DJI's paternal interference in its customers' flight plans probably will reduce unintentional incidents like last week's White House landing. But it certainly won't prevent the scenario feared by official Washington: an attacker looking to weaponize a drone. For one thing, hardcore drone hobbyists tend to be tinkerers, and sooner or later their rumbling will translate into published firmware hacks and workarounds anyone can use.

"Right now there doesn't exist any hacks to remove the geofencing or downgrade the firmware," says Herbert. "I'm sure they're coming. People will figure it out eventually."

But, he notes, drone fliers who don't want geofencing have many options. DJI's mandatory update only affects the Phantom 2 line— ironically, the older Phantom 1 that landed at the White House isn't included. And Phantom 2 owners will receive the mandatory update only when they link their drone to their Internet-connected PC or Mac. And if you really want to exercise your own judgment when flying, DJI says you can simply buy from a competitor.

"We do provide different layers of security to make it difficult to hack and get around," says DJI's Perry. But for those determined to avoid geofencing, "there's an easy way to do that, which is to buy another quad-copter."

That may be true for now, but it's easy to see lawmakers and regulators jumping on DJI's mandatory update as an easy cure, and mandating geofencing industrywide. When that happens, you can expect that circumventing drone firmware, for any reason, will become illegal, the same way hacking your car's programming is illegal. One thing is for certain: Nobody willing to strap a bomb to a toy drone will be deterred.

Drones Can Easily Get Out of Control

Robert Stone

Robert Stone holds a chair in interactive multimedia systems within the College of Engineering and Physical Sciences at the University of Birmingham, where he is also director of the Human Interface Technologies (HIT) Team.

M ini drones are not yet appearing in our skies on a daily basis but they certainly are a rapidly growing trend. People can and do get hurt so we really need to help amateur pilots learn how to fly their new toys safely.

There are all kinds of exciting developments happening in this field and hobbyists are now able to pick up a device for relatively little money. But as more and more of these devices come onto the market, more grisly images are popping up online to show what happens when people lose control.

My team and I have been experimenting with drones for some months, flying them over hard-to-reach heritage sites but, as our experience of deploying these platforms has increased, we have become increasingly concerned about how they can be used safely.

Many of the promises about what we will use drones for in the near future are just flights of fancy, especially given the limited payload capabilities of most commercial off-the-shelf products, but the technology is certainly evolving fast.

Out of control?

The main limiting factor for a drone is often the untrained pilot at its helm. There have certainly been incidents in the recent past which demonstrate the consequences of human error, system failure, flying in inappropriate weather conditions and sheer incompetence.

Earlier this year, a resident of Barrow-in-Furness was prosecuted for flying a radio-controlled aircraft in restricted airspace over BAE Systems' nuclear submarine facility. A similar incident occurred in May when a man was was questioned by the FBI for crashing a camera-equipped sUAV close to the Bridgeport Harbour Electricity Generating Station in Conneticut. No one was injured in either case but both represented pretty serious incidents in terms of flying within restricted airspace.

There have been numerous reports of injuries, even fatalities, caused by loss of control of an sUAV and some pretty harrowing images can easily be found online. Reported cases include a bridegroom who was struck in the face by a quadcopter flown by an adventurous wedding photographer, and the crashing of a hexacopter into the grandstand at Virginia Motorsports Park, injuring five. The second half of 2013 was particularly bad, with fatalities in Texas, Korea and Brazil and the horrendous case of a 19-year-old who died instantly in a Brooklyn park when the blades of his radio controlled aircraft struck his head and neck.

Of course, there are rules and guidelines about drones. But when the Civil Aviation Authority tries to address the human factor in its guidelines, its efforts fall rather flat. Its warnings are far too generic and rigid to cope with a rapidly changing technological scene. It discusses the dangers of remote data feedback and stresses that it's important for pilots to remain situationally aware, but the style of wording and absence of illustrated examples do little to emphasise the very real dangers of flying when non-expert pilots are in charge of a drone.

Having now experimented with a number of drones at historical sites, often in remote moorland or coastal regions, I find myself in strong agreement with those who call for regulations to be strengthened. Indeed, we have recently produced our own Standard Operating Procedures in an attempt to fill in the gaps evident in existing guidance.

Over the past 12 months alone, our hexacopter has evolved from a 2kg to 4kg payload capacity. Our students have, as a result, been able to experiment with different tools for the drones. One has been a camera that feeds video back to a headed mounted display worn by the pilot on the ground. This certainly generates impressive video but even our experienced pilot has been "drawn in" by the stunning picture quality, only to be alerted—just in time —to the appearance of the sUAV propeller blades in his field of view as the vehicle becomes progressively unstable.

Flying school

It is possible to take training courses for flying drones but these often tend to be aimed at those wanting to use sUAVs for professional or commercial work, as opposed to the hobbyist or academic researcher. It is clear that, as the stories of injuries, fatalities, property damage, invasion of privacy, trespass and airspace incursion multiply, the situation has to change, even though any change will, without doubt, be very unpopular with many hobbyists and retailers.

Some developers have started working on firmware modifications that would help pilots stop their drones from inadvertently flying into restricted airspace. This is a promising development, even if it might not be met with great enthusiasm from users, but much more needs to be done. Every drone sold needs to be registered and marked (perhaps even chipped) in some way so that it can be traced directly back to its owner if something goes wrong. There is no doubt that this will be difficult to enforce, especially as 3D printing technologies are increasingly being used to manufacture replacement components.

Drone pilots also need to submit to some form of basic competence assessment, such as through an app, and should then be granted a licence. Such an assessment could take the form of a test similar to those used to teach driving students about decision-making and observational skills.

sUAV simulator packages already exist, as do apps, but most fall short of teaching and evaluating the essential skills and awareness necessary for safe sUAV operations. We should focus on human-centred design issues from the start so that simulators can test reaction times, decision-making for flights in urban or sensitive areas, pilot distraction effects and other potential problems a pilot might face.

Of course, such tests would not replace professional courses but they would help to ensure that the growing number of pilots can fly their devices safely. Some might complain that these measures are over the top and totally unnecessary for something that is, after all, just a smaller version of a radio controlled helicopter. But just type "quadcopter injuries" into Google images and make your own mind up.

Drones Are Unlikely to Interfere with Air Traffic

David Schneider

David Schneider is senior editor at IEEE Spectrum. *He previously worked for* Scientific American *and* American Scientist.

L ast December, a group of investors called the UAS America Fund petitioned the Federal Aviation Administration to create a set of rules that would govern "micro unmanned aircraft." The basic idea is that these microdrones—defined as being 3 pounds (1.4 kilograms) and under—pose much less of a hazard than many of the model aircraft now flying in the United States, which can weigh as much as 55 pounds (25 kilograms). So it makes no sense to regulate all "small unmanned aircraft systems," as the FAA likes to call them, the same way, which might well be what the U.S. government has in store.

While the rules the investment group has drafted make for an interesting read, what I found particularly eye-opening was an attached report from Exponent, a failure-analysis consultancy. That report tries to quantify the threat such microdrones—a category that includes popular models like the DJI Phantom and 3DR Iris—would pose to full-scale aircraft using data the FAA has collected on collisions with birds.

Bird strikes, as these incidents are called, have plagued aviation since its inception. And that's not surprising. There are a lot of birds—10 billion in the United States, according to Exponent—and some of them get quite large. You only have to think back to the dramatic goose-caused ditching of US Airways Flight 1549 in the Hudson River in 2009 to realize that birds are more than a theoretical threat.

"Smaller Drones Aren't Major Threat to Aircraft: A Little Birdie Told Me So," David Schneider, *IEEE Spectrum*, January 28, 2015. Reprinted by permission.

Fortunatcly, the aviation industry and regulators have found ways to reduce these natural hazards. For example, airports use a type of grass that geese don't particularly like to eat. And aircraft are subject to various regulations about how robust they have to be in the face of something like a goose flying into the blades of a jet turbine.

That's not to say that the aviation industry has this problem licked. By no means. Bird strikes are a very real threat to aviators and their passengers. But as Exponent's report aptly shows, the severity of the danger scales with the size of the bird, which only makes sense.

US Airways Flight 1549, for example, suffered crippling damage to its engines on takeoff after it ran into a flock of Canadian geese, which can weigh as much as 18 pounds (8 kilograms). And there are plenty of other examples of other large birds—pelicans, vultures, cranes, and so forth—creating similar havoc in the air, sometimes with tragic results.

But Exponent's examination of the FAA's wildlife-strike database reveals something interesting. The smaller classes of birds documented there (those the size of sparrows or gulls) rarely cause aviation fatalities. Indeed, the FAA's database, which records incidents back to 1990, lists only three fatal accidents attributed to small or medium-size birds, according to the Exponent report. And a deeper examination of those three accidents casts considerable doubt on whether a collision with smallish birds really caused two of the three.

The earliest of these three fatal accidents took place in 1994. According to the ensuing report of the National Transportation Safety Board, the helicopter involved crashed not because of an actual collision with one or more birds, but because the pilot took aggressive evasive actions to avoid a flock of birds and inadvertently overstressed his aircraft. The rotor then struck the tail boom, and the helicopter dropped out of the sky.

The second of the three fatal incidents took place in 1998. Here it was a fixed-wing aircraft involved. Two people flying in the plane died. Thankfully, the plane killed no one on the ground, despite crashing into the roof of New Jersey condo. The type of bird responsible for this tragedy remains unknown. Actually, investigators are not at all sure there really was a bird involved.

The evidence for some sort of avian component to this accident consists of one witness's report that she saw a large number of birds flying in the area. There was some enigmatic damage to a portion of the plane's horizontal stabilizer, but no bird feathers, blood, or remains were found on the plane. Swabbing by ornithologists called in to examine the wreckage failed to turn up bird DNA. And after reviewing the relevant photos, the Air Force's Bird/Wildlife Aircraft Strike Hazard Team, like the ornithologists, demurred in attributing the damage to a bird strike.

This leaves only one more fatal accident in the FAA database that has been ascribed to a small or medium-size bird. This one, the crash of a helicopter ferrying oil-field workers to offshore platforms in the Gulf of Mexico, took place in 2009. Two pilots and six of the seven passengers died.

Although there was no obvious evidence of a bird strike on initial inspection of the wreckage, swabs sent to the Smithsonian Institution's feather-identification lab turned up DNA from a female red-tailed hawk. Such birds generally weigh a kilogram or perhaps slightly more (say, 2 to 3 pounds), so it's surprising at least to me that a collision with something this small would be enough to take down a helicopter. The National Transportation Safety Board's summary of this accident hints at a complicating factor, however: a windshield that might not have been up to par.

You see, the company running this helicopter-ferry service had had issues with the stock glass windshields on its helicopters delaminating, so they replaced them with aftermarket acrylic windshields, which according to the NTSB report hadn't been tested for their resistance to bird strikes. And an identical acrylic windshield installed in a different helicopter allowed a colliding gull to pass right through it three years earlier. But that incident hadn't caused this obviously fragile windshield design to be removed from service generally.

So some bird strikes can be darn dangerous. But despite that fact, and despite the enormous numbers of these creatures zooming around the sky, only very rarely do collisions with smaller varieties of birds kill people. Less serious accidents aren't, however, uncommon.

According to the Exponent study, the FAA's database has a total of 150,000 entries, and out of those, there are 13,906 reports that note damage from small or medium birds. And there are 227 incidents noted that had non-fatal injuries. Of course, we have no idea how many inconsequential bird strikes go unreported. So it's hard to judge odds of a bird strike being significant from these numbers.

What's more, if you only consider small- and medium-size bird strikes that occurred in places where microdrones would be likely allowed (below 400 feet altitude and more than 5 miles from an airport), the results don't look at all alarming: the Exponent report says there have been zero fatalities and at most a handful of accidents with injuries.

This is all to say that drones of about a kilogram or so in mass would likely pose little danger, so long as people flew them away from where full-size aircraft are allowed to fly. (In the United States, piloted aircraft are supposed to fly above either 500 feet or 1000 feet above ground level, depending on how densely the area is populated.)

So why not let drones of a size that pose comparatively little danger fly without imposing onerous restrictions on them? Any flub-ups that bring a full-sized aircraft and a microdrone to the same area and altitude are bound to be no more worrisome than the situation equivalently sized birds have long put aviators in. And we've somehow put up with that.

Drones Offer Numerous Benefits and Few Risks

Pierluigi Paganini

Pierluigi Paganini is chief information security officer at Bit4Id and a member of the ENISA (European Union Agency for Network and Information Security)Treat Landscape Stakeholder Group. He is also a security evangelist, security analyst, and freelance writer.

I n December, Amazon.com, the world's largest online retailer, announced that it is testing unmanned drones to deliver products ordered by its customers. The service was experimental, and it could probably take up to five years to start. In discussion is the possibility to adopt unmanned aerial vehicles (UAV) for civil use. As explained by the CEO of Amazon, Jeff Bezos, the introduction of UAVs in the supply chain of the company can bring many benefits, exactly as in many other sectors.

"We can do half-hour delivery…and we can carry objects, we think, up to five pounds (2.3kg), which covers 86% of the items that we deliver," said Bezos.

The drone industry is growing at a rapid pace. Aerospace research company Teal Group has estimated that sales of military and civilian drones will total over $89 billion in the next 10 years. The possible fields of application for UAVs are unlimited. Some of the most interesting usages could be grouped in the following categories.

Protection of population

This category can include services like firefighting and wildfire detection, disaster relief, search and rescue. In all the above scenarios, drones could operate in risky areas or could be deployed to monitor specific areas to prevent incidents or to provide all the

"Privacy and Security Issues for the Usage of Civil Drones," Pierluigi Paganini, resources. infosecinstitute.com, April 25, 2014.

necessary support to the forces of intervention in the event of environmental disasters or accidents.

Using UAVs, supplies can be transported rapidly into critical areas requiring medical attention, or any other kind of support, including food rations and other medicines. Drones can also be used by firefighting squads to monitor the progression of fires in wide areas, avoiding the need to involve civil personnel, or can be exploited to locate missing persons.

UAVs could be equipped with thermal sensors or night vision cameras, and they can be used to quickly inspect a wide area, providing detailed information on it to the control center.

Mineral prospection and mining
Drones equipped with specific sensors can cover in-flight large areas for mineral detection. UAVs can be used to build a map of the territory by analyzing the rock composition. Large areas with differing elevations could be inspected with high accuracy on a regular basis.

Agriculture
The agriculture industry is one of the sectors that most of all is benefiting of UAV usage, drones can rapidly map the fields, and could be also used to spray the crops with water or to fertilize the fields.

Construction and infrastructure inspection
Drones could be used to monitor critical infrastructure in a large area, taking pictures of pipelines, bridges and power lines. The goal is to support maintenance activities and assess the structures. In the near future, drones could be used to also operate reparations to minimize the risk of any injury to human workers.

No doubt, drone usage will bring different benefits but also raise numerous implications under security and privacy perspectives. Amazon is just one of numerous companies that will use unmanned aerial vehicles for civilian purposes. The US Federal Aviation Administration (FAA) has approved their use for police and government agencies, issuing about 1,400 permits over the past several years, and it will authorize civilian air space use by 2015. The situation is quite similar in Europe, where the use of drones for civilian use is expected to start by 2016.

The principal risks are represented by the possibility that groups of criminals and cyber terrorists could hack unmanned aerial vehicles, with intent of harming the population. Drones could be attacked for several purposes, and hackers could be intentioned to interfere with the services they provide and could abuse them for cyber espionage or could hijack them for sabotage.

The difficulties of the commercial drone industry

The U.S. commercial drone industry is slow to take off, more than two years after President Obama signed into law a bill that authorizes the civilian use of unmanned aerial vehicles in the country.

The Federal Aviation Administration Modernization and Reform Act of 2012 authorizes the FAA to issue licenses for commercial drone use in the U.S, and at the same time, request to the agency to define rules for the usage of civilian drones by private entities and by law enforcement agencies.

While the central government approved the law for use of commercial drones, since it was passed in February 2012, nearly 43 states have proposed a total of 130 bills and resolutions seeking limits on drone use to avoid privacy and civil rights violations.

The technologies which equip the drones could be abused to spy on unaware individuals. Privacy and civil liberties advocates have raised many doubts about the legitimacy of facial recognition cameras, thermal imaging cameras, open Wi-Fi sniffers, license plate scanners and other sensors.

To better understand the limitation imposed by lawmakers, let's consider the proposal originated in the states of Louisiana and Pennsylvania, which ban the use of UAVs in certain circumstances.

The Louisiana state legislature is considering two separate proposals to ban the use of commercial drones. The first one to prohibit drones from flying over critical infrastructure (e.g. Chemical plants, water treatment facilities, gas and oil storage and delivery facilities, telecommunications networks). The second proposed bill aimed to prohibit private drone operators from capturing images of individuals or of private property without explicit permission.

The above proposal resumed the principal concerns related to the involvement of drones in civil and private activities. Overseas the situation also appears confused. In Europe, the use of drones is increasing for a wide variety of purposes, including crop monitoring, traffic management and news reporting.

The use of drones for civil uses is syndicated for two main reasons. The risk that these machines could be hijacked or can be subjected to failure, and for the fear that they could collect unauthorized data, violating privacy of citizens. The FAA has announced that one of its top priorities is to publish rules for small UAVs later this year.

"The rulemaking is very complex, and we want to ensure that we strike the right balance of requirements for small [drones] to help foster growth in this emerging industry," an FAA spokeswoman said in an email.

The European Commission has recently proposed to set tough new standards to regulate the operations of drones for civil usage. According to the work of the Commission, the new standards must cover safety, security, privacy, data protection, insurance and liability.

The principal problem is the fragmentation of law across the EU. In Europe, basic national safety rules are applied and it is important to uniform them within a share regulatory.

"Civil drones can check for damage on road and rail bridges, monitor natural disasters such as flooding and spray crops with pinpoint accuracy. They come in all shapes and sizes. In the future they may even deliver books from your favourite online retailer. But many people, including myself, have concerns about the safety, security and privacy issues relating to these devices," said Vice-President Siim Kallas, Commissioner for mobility and transport.

Europe is looking at the technology for civil drones as a business and economic opportunity that could bring operational advantages and job creation. The sector in the next 10 years could be worth 10% of the aviation market—that's €15 billion per year.

"If ever there was a right time to do this, and to do this at a European level, it is now. Because remotely piloted aircraft, almost by definition, are going to cross borders and the industry is still in its infancy. We have an opportunity now to make a single set of rules that everyone can work with, just like we do for larger aircraft."

The new standards requested by the European Commission will cover the following areas:

- Strict EU wide rules on safety authorisations.
- Tough controls on privacy and data protection.
- Controls to ensure security.
- A clear framework for liability and insurance.
- Streamlining R&D and supporting new industry.

Privacy concerns, drones as a spyware tool

It is not difficult to imagine how to use drones for cyber espionage. These vehicles are very flexible and could be used to control targets remotely, but one of most interesting uses could be the usage of UAVs to interfere with target communications.

A couple of months ago, researchers at the London-based Sensepoint security firm designed a software that, once deployed on a drone, allow the vehicle to steal data from mobile devices surrounding it.

The potentialities of such applications are infinite. Imagine a victim walking around looking for an open Wi-Fi network while a UAV is flying over his head. The attacker is able to steal data from the victim's handset.

The application, called Snoopy, runs on drones and looks for a smartphone signal while it is searching for a Wi-Fi network. The software is designed to trick a victim's mobile device into thinking it's connecting to a trusted access point to access data from the handset once attached.

Snoopy could be used by attackers to steal a victim's data, including user credentials, credit card numbers and location data. The researchers at Sensepoint successfully demonstrated the ability of the Snoopy application to steal Amazon, PayPal, and Yahoo credentials from random citizens while the drone was flying over their heads in the streets of London.

The unique possibility that potential victims have to protect their data is to turn off any automatic connection process, including the Wi-Fi network-finding feature.

EU secret surveillance drone project

A document recently issued by rights group Statewatch, titled "Eurodrones Inc.," reports that the EU is secretly investing into surveillance drone projects without knowledge of citizens.

"More than 315 million euro ($430 million) has so far been spent in EU research funding on drone technology or drones geared towards a specific purpose such as policing or border control," states the report.

According to the report, the EU is secretly promoting "the further militarization" of the region with a series of research funding "invisible" to the people and parliaments of Europe. The report claims the total lack of proper political oversight. It seems that many projects were financed with investments on the EU legislation on air traffic control for this year.

"The EU's emerging drone policy has come about following years of successful lobbying by defense and security companies and their associates," said co-author of the report Chris Jones in a statement on Statewatch's website.

The projects referred to in the document would engage in civilian surveillance activities, such as border patrols, and the possible use of drones in the fight against illicit activities. The Statewatch group is mainly concerned by the secret nature of the program that could hide further purposes in the development of the drone program, like a "further militarization" of the European Union.

The report also highlights that none of the civil organizations, including the European Group on Ethics, the LIBE Committee of the European Parliament or the European Agency for Fundamental Rights and Data Protection Supervisor, were involved in a public debate on the issue.

"Yet none of these bodies have been involved…Their absence from policy debates means that many of the conversations the EU should be having about drones—such as what they should and should not be used for, and how to prevent further militarization and the deployment of fully autonomous weaponized drones— have been all but ignored," is reported in the document.

It's important to highlight that the authors of the report are not averse to the use of drones in the research into a new generation of unmanned aerial vehicles, but they do stress the fact that the current investments are covert to the EU population for "the interests of the big defense contractors."

The group is very concerned for civil liberties. The uncontrolled development of drones for civil use could lead to "unwarranted state surveillance and repression."

The fear of sabotage

Civil drones could be abused not only for surveillance purposes, they could be hijacked or destroyed by attackers, causing the interruption of the service they provide. Drones can obviously be killed, but one of most fascinating concerns is related to the possibility that they can be hacked.

In the last months security expert Samy Kamkar designed a software dubbed SkyJack to allow an attacker to gain control over a drone while it's still flying.

Kamkar published the details on his website, the researcher defined SkyJack as the "Zombie drone," and the software runs on a Parrot AR.Drone 2 and is able to scan for wireless signals of other UAVs in the vicinity.

The choice of this specific drone is not casual, it has been estimated that 500,000 Parrot drones were placed on the market since 2010. Theoretically anyone can create its own UAV to hunt down other drones and control them.

SkyJack was presented in the same period Amazon announced its intention to use drones for shipping its products and Kamkar referred to the critical aspect of security for civil usage of UAVs.

"How fun would it be to take over drones, carrying Amazon packages…or take over any other drones and make them my little zombie drones…Awesome." Kamkar asked rhetorically in his blog post

To demonstrate how SkyJack works when it finds other drones nearby, Zombie drone interferes with the target drone's wireless connection in attempt to disconnect it from its control center. Once it has disconnected the targeted drone from the base station, Zombie drone takes the operator's place, gaining full control of the victim UAV.

As explained by Kamkar in his post, SkyJack uses a radio-controlled Parrot AR.Drone quadcopter equipped with a Raspberry Pi circuit board, a small battery, and two wireless transmitters.

The Zombie drones run a custom software designed by the hacker and also off-the-shelf applications that are used to scan wireless connections of nearby UAVs. SkyJack analyzed the media access control (MAC) addresses of all Wi-Fi devices within its radio range. Once he detected a MAC address belonging to a block of addresses used by Parrot AR.Drone vehicles, he exploited the open-source Aircrack-ng app for Wi-Fi hacking to issue a command that disconnects the target UAV from the mobile handset currently being used to control and monitor it. Now the attacker is able to gain control of the drone.

"Using a Parrot AR.Drone 2, a Raspberry Pi, a USB battery, an Alfa AWUS036H wireless transmitter, aircrack-ng, node-ar-drone, node.js, and my SkyJack software, I developed a drone that flies around, seeks the wireless signal of any other drone in the area, forcefully disconnects the wireless connection of the true owner of the target drone, then authenticates with the target drone pretending to be its owner, then feeds commands to it and all other possessed zombie drones at my will," said KamKar.

Another interesting attack scenario hypothesized by Kamkar is include a version of SkyJack that runs on grounded Linux machines that is able to hack drones within radio range without need of any drone.

"SkyJack also works when grounded as well, no drone is necessary on your end for it to work. You can simply run it from your own Linux machine/Raspberry Pi/laptop/etc and jack drones straight out of the sky."

At the moment, SkyJack is designed only to attack a small range of drones having their MACs fall inside an address block reserved by Parrot AR.Drone vehicles, but it could be easily adapted to target other families of drones.

Preventing this kind of attack is not difficult. In this specific case, it is possible to use a secret key to provide mutual authentication between the controller and the drone, and using the key each command message sent could be enciphered.

The athlete injured by "hacked" camera drone

A few weeks ago, a drone operated by a film company crashed onto the course of an Australian triathlon, injuring one athlete, Raji Ogden. The operator reported that suddenly he lost control of the vehicles because someone deliberately jammed his wireless control link.

The operator of the drone, Warren Abrams of New Era Photography and Film, reported that an attacker using a "channel hop" attack succeeded to gain complete control of the drone. He also referred to having suffered other anomalies in the drone control in the same day.

The above incident is the result of a typical attack against the communication link of the drone. Wi-Fi Jamming is a possible attack that could cause the loss of control of the aerial vehicle with serious consequences for nearby people.

The concerning aspect of such attacks is that they can be carried out with off-shelf products. In some cases, just a simple mobile is enough if the drone was operating on an unsecured Wi-Fi network.

Flying drones can be easily crashed using cheap tools available on the market. An attacker could use them to interfere with UAVs. These tools include GPS jammers and do-it-yourself high energy radio frequency guns that could be used to destroy the communication link with the drone, and in the best case, to force the secure landing of the vehicles.

New Zealand security researcher Stuart MacIntosh told delegates at the Kiwicon 7 conference in Wellington last year that some vulnerable drone technology designed in the hobby space had trickled down into use by police and commercial operators.

"It meant a variety of drones were open to attacks that could destabilise or crash the aircraft."

"You can walk all over [the Parrot AR Drone] with frequency-hopping spread spectrum ... you can fly a radio plane near an AR drone and it will very quickly get packet loss... A lot of these UAVs (unmanned aerial vehicles) were not really designed with security in mind apart from some that may be destined for law enforcement use or military use...You can build your own [GPS] jammer or buy one off eBay for $100 with free shipping," said MacIntosh.

Conclusions

One of principal problems in the approach to cyber security for civil drones is the great confusion in emerging government regulation. The terms "drone" and "unmanned aircraft system" (UAS) are often confused and are used in imprecise ways. The FAA, for example, use the term "UAS" to refer to both armed military aircraft and toys including model aircraft. The FAA agency has made little distinction between possible uses of UAS and the categories of users authorized to deploy "drones" for their activities. Actual trends seem to suggest that any commercial activity is considered illegal.

"In response to this growing demand for public use unmanned aircraft operations, the FAA developed guidance in a Memorandum titled "Unmanned Aircraft Systems Operations in the U.S. National Airspace System—Interim Operational Approval Guidance" (UAS Policy 05-01). In this document, the FAA set out guidance for public use of unmanned aircraft by defining a process for evaluating applications for Certificate(s) of Waiver or Authorization (COA's) for unmanned aircraft to operate in the National Airspace System. The concern was not only that unmanned aircraft operations might interfere with 3 commercial and general aviation aircraft operations, but that they could also pose a safety problem for other airborne vehicles, and persons or property on the ground."

The various attack scenarios against civil drones described in this paper highlight the importance of cyber security for these complex vehicles. Foreign governments and cyber terrorists could exploit the technology to hit a country and its infrastructure. It is necessary to set a maximum level of alert for UAV manufacturers. In the next years these technologies will be largely used for different purposes. UAVs will crowd the sky and security must be the first requirement to ensure safety and privacy of the population. It is a hard challenge to face with cyber threats growing ever more complex, that's why it is absolutely a joint effort of manufacturers, industry, and security firms, government, private companies and of course of the common people to be aware of abilities and risks of the technology.

Organizations to Contact

The editors have compiled the following list of organizations concerned with the issues debated in this book. The descriptions are derived from materials provided by the organizations. All have publications or information available for interested readers. This list was compiled on the date of publication of the present volume; the information provided here may change. Be aware that many organizations take several weeks or longer to respond to inquiries, so allow as much time as possible.

Association for Unmanned Vehicle Systems International

2700 S. Quincy Street, Suite 400, Arlington, VA 22206
(703) 845-9671
website: www.auvsi.org/home

The Association for Unmanned Vehicle Systems International (AUVSI) is the world's largest nonprofit organization devoted exclusively to advancing the unmanned systems and robotics community. Serving more than 7,500 members from government organizations, industry, and academia, AUVSI is committed to fostering, developing, and promoting unmanned systems and robotics technologies. AUVSI members support the defense, civil, and commercial sectors.

Drone Advocates For Public Safety

P.O. Box 2344, Decatur, GA 30031
email: info@droneadvocates.org
website: http://www.droneadvocates.org/get-a-grant

The mission of Drone Advocates for Public Safety is to reduce injuries, deaths, and economic damage by ensuring public safety organizations gain access to the newest aerial safety technology. The organization provides flight training to first responders, educates the public about drone safety, works with lawmakers and regulatory agencies, and acts as a liaison between tech companies and first responder agencies to drive innovation.

Drone Pilots Association (DPA)
website: http://dronepilotsassociation.com

The DPA's mission is to be a single entity that represents the interests of all small commercial and non-hobbyist drone pilots. There are several entities that represent specific sectors of commercial drone operations. The intent of the DPA is to represent all of those sectors, regardless of the type of commercial or non-hobbyist operations.

Federal Aviation Administration
800 Independence Avenue SW, Washington, DC 20591
(866) 835-5322
website: www.faa.gov

As part of the US Department of Transportation, the Federal Aviation Administration is the national aviation authority of the United States. The FAA oversees airports, air traffic, commercial space vehicles, and commercial aircraft, including drones. The agency seeks to provide the safest, most efficient aerospace system in the world.

Know Before You Fly
email: contact@knowbeforeyoufly.org
website: http://knowbeforeyoufly.org

Know Before You Fly is an education campaign founded by the Association for Unmanned Vehicle Systems International (AUVSI) and the Academy of Model Aeronautics (AMA) in partnership with the Federal Aviation Administration (FAA) to educate prospective users about the safe and responsible operation of unmanned aircraft systems (UAS). Know Before You Fly provides prospective users with the information and guidance they need to fly safely and responsibly.

UAV Systems Association (UAVSA)
(866) 691-7776
email: info@uavsa.org
website: www.uavsa.org

UAVSA supplies its members with information, tools, and resources to engage and inform the community and help sUAS businesses to succeed. Founded in 2014, UAVSA offers members key partnerships, provides a community, and hosts nationwide events, including the annual International Drone Expo.

UAVUS
4880 Lower Roswell Road, Suite 165-505, Marietta, GA 30068
(770) 299-9602
email: support@uavus.org
website: http://uavus.org

UAVUS is the largest association of civil and civic commercial UAV operators in the United States. The organization advocates for the commercial use of small UAVs for aerial imaging and creates value for independent, professional unmanned aerial videographers. It is the mission of UAVUS to educate lawmakers on the benefits of commercial UAVs for aerial imaging and introduce technologies that enable safe operations and to create public relations and education campaigns that illustrate the professionalism and high standards of UAVUS members.

US Drone Racing Association (USDRA)
email: usdra@pobox.com
website: http://usdra.org

The goal of the USDRA is to bring the sport of remote controlled multirotor first-person view (FPV) UAVs into the mainstream. The association aims to promote the sport of FPV drone racing, provide safety guidelines, serve as a resource for the public on the terminology and ideas behind drone racing, and work with the drone community to develop guidelines for races, meets, and fair competition.

Veterans for Peace
1404 North Broadway
St. Louis, MO 63102
(314) 725-6005
email: vfp@veteransforpeace.org
website: www.veteransforpeace.org/our-work/join-working-group/drones-robots-and-future-weapons-working-group

The Veterans for Peace working group on drones has been established to become knowledgeable about drones and related weapons; educate the public about the issues created by the use of drones and robots as weapons and surveillance tools; end the development, production, and use of drones through coordinated efforts with other like-minded groups and individuals; end targeted assassinations; and defend the right to privacy and freedom by banning information-gathering of citizens and others, by drones and advanced surveillance systems.

Bibliography

Books

Akbar Ahmed. *The Thistle and the Drone: How America's War on Terror Became a Global War on Tribal Islam.* Washington, DC: Brookings Institution, 2013.

Peter L. Bergen and Daniel Rothenberg. *Drone Wars: Transforming Conflict, Law, and Policy.* New York, NY: Cambridge University Press, 2015.

Laurie Calhoun. *We Kill Because We Can.* London, UK: Zed Books, 2015.

Gregoire Chamayou and Janet Lloyd. *Drone Theory.* London: Penguin Books, 2015.

Noam Chomsky and Andre Vitchek. *On Western Terrorism: From Hiroshima to Drone Warfare.* New York, NY: Palgrave Macmillan, 2013.

Lloyd C. Gardner. *Killing Machine: The American Presidency in the Age of Drone Warfare.* New York, NY: The New Press, 2013.

John J. Kaag and Sarah E. Kreps. *Drone Warfare.* Cambridge, UK: Polity Press, 2014.

Avery Plaw, Matthew S. Fricker, and Carlos R. Colon. *The Drone Debate: A Primer on the U.S. Use of Unmanned Aircraft Outside Conventional Battlefields.* Lanham, MD: Rowman & Littlefield, 2015.

Jefferson Powell. *Targeting Americans: The Constituionality of the U.S. Drone War.* New York, NY: Oxford University Press, 2016.

Nancy Robinson Masters. *Drone Pilot.* Ann Arbor, MI: Cherry Lake Publishers, 2013.

Ann Rogers and John Hill. *Unmanned: Drone Warfare and Global Security*. New York, NY: Pluto Press, 2014.

Adam Rothstein. *Drone*. New York, NY: Bloomsbury Academic, 2015.

Erik Rudaski, James Igoe Walsh, and Jeremiah Gertler. *Drone Strikes: Effectiveness, Consequences and Unmanned Aerial Systems Background*. New York, NY: Nova Science Publishers, 2014.

Jeremy Scahill. *The Assassination Complex: Inside the Government's Secret Drone Warfare Program*. New York, NY: Simon & Schuster, 2016.

Scott Shane. *Objective Troy: A Terrorist, a President, and the Rise of the Drone*. New York, NY: Tim Duggan Books, 2015.

Dave Sloggett. *Drone Warfare: The Development of Unmanned Aerial Conflict*. New York, NY: Skyhorse Publishing, 2014.

Bradley Jay Strawser. *Opposing Perspectives on the Drone Debate*. New York, NY: Palgrave Macmillan, 2014.

Richard Whittle. *Predator: The Secret Origins of the Drone Revolution*. New York, NY: Henry Holt and Company, 2014.

Brian Glyn Williams. *Predators: The CIA's Drone War on al Qaeda*. Washington, DC: Potomac Books, 2013.

Chris Woods. *Sudden Justice: America's Secret Drone Wars*. New York, NY: Oxford University Press, 2015.

Periodicals and Internet Sources

Wells C. Bennett. "Civilian Drones, Privacy and the Federal-State Balance," Brookings Institute, September 2014. https://www.brookings.edu/research/civilian-drones-privacy-and-the-federal-state-balance.

Mark Bowden. "The Killing Machines," *Atlantic*, September 2013. http://www.theatlantic.com/magazine/

archive/2013/09/the-killing-machines-how-to-think-about-drones/309434.

CBS News. "Drones: Eyes in the Sky," CBS news, May 16, 2013. http://www.cbsnews.com/news/drones-eyes-in-the-sky.

Steve Coll. "The Unblinking Stare," *New Yorker,* November 24, 2014. http://www.newyorker.com/magazine/2014/11/24/unblinking-stare.

Economist. "Those Incredible Flying Machines," *Economist,* June 25, 2016. http://www.economist.com/news/science-and-technology/21701080-personal-robotic-aircraft-are-cheaper-and-safer-helicopterand-much-easier

Economist. "Welcome to the Drone Age," *The Economist,* September 26, 2015. http://www.economist.com/news/science-and-technology/21666118-miniature-pilotless-aircraft-are-verge-becoming-commonplace-welcome.

Conor Friedersdorf. "Eyes over Compton: How Police Spied on a Whole City," *Atlantic,* April 21, 2014. http://www.theatlantic.com/national/archive/2014/04/sheriffs-deputy-compares-drone-surveillance-of-compton-to-big-brother/360954.

Andy Greenberg. "Hacker Says He Can Hijack a $35K Police Drone a Mile Away," *Wired,* March 2, 2016. https://www.wired.com/2016/03/hacker-says-can-hijack-35k-police-drone-mile-away.

Steven Groves. "Drone Strikes: The Legality of U.S. Targeting Terrorists Abroad," Heritage Foundation, April 10, 2013. http://www.heritage.org/research/reports/2013/04/drone-strikes-the-legality-of-us-targeting-terrorists-abroad.

Chad C. Haddal and Jeremiah Gertler. "Homeland Security: Unmanned Aerial Vehicles and Border Surveillance," CRS Report for Congress, July 8, 2010. http://trac.syr.edu/immigration/library/P4798.pdf.

Jason Hanna. "Targeting terrorists with bombs and bullets," CNN, September 23, 2015. http://www.cnn.com/ interactive/2014/09/world/us-terror-groups.

Michael C. Heatherly. "Drones: The American Controversy," Journal of Strategic Security, USF Libraries at Scholar Commons. http://scholarcommons.usf.edu/cgi/viewcontent. cgi?article=1387&context=jss.

Jeanne M. Hill. "Drones: The Latest Threat to the Right to Privacy," National Judicial College, July 16, 2015. http:// www.judges.org/drones-latest-threat-right-privacy.

Joan Lowy. "Civilian Drones Are Causing Problems For Pilots," businessinsider.com, Nov 12, 2014. http://www. businessinsider.com/civilian-drones-are-causing-problems-for-pilots-2014-11.

Stephen Maddox and David Stuckenberg. "Drones in the U.S. National Airspace System: A Safety and Security Assessment," *Harvard Law School National Security Journal*, February 24, 2015. http://harvardnsj.org/2015/02/drones-in-the-u-s-national-airspace-system-a-safety-and-security-assessment.

Andrea Noel. "Tunnels, Drones, Jet Skis, and Planes: How the Cartels Beat a Border Wall," *Daily Beast*, September 17, 2015. http://www.thedailybeast.com/articles/2016/09/17/cartel-watch-a-border-wall-won-t-keep-out-the-cartels. html.

Paul D. Shinkman. "Tomorrow's Wars and the American Cybersoldiers Who Will Fight Them," *U.S. News & World Report*, August 29, 2016. http://www.usnews.com/news/articles/2016-08-29/tomorrows-wars-and-the-american-cybersoldiers-who-will-fight-them.

Andrew Soergel. "New Application for Drones: Disaster Relief," *U.S. News & World Report*, June 23, 2016. http://www.

usnews.com/news/articles/2016-06-23/new-application-for-drones-disaster-relief.

Caspar van Vark. "Drones Set to Give Global Farming a Makeover," *Guardian*, December 26, 2015. https://www.theguardian.com/global-development/2015/dec/26/drones-farming-crop-problems-uavs.

Nick Wingfield. "A Field Guide to Civilian Drones," *New York Times*, August 29, 2016. http://www.nytimes.com/interactive/2015/technology/guide-to-civilian-drones.html?_r=0.

Index